When On The Road To
Enlightenment, Don't Forget To
Take Out The Trash

When On The Road To Enlightenment, Don't Forget To Take Out The Trash

Kellie Fitzgerald

IbbiLane Press

IbbiLane Press

Copyright © 2014 by Kellie Fitzgerald

All rights reserved. No part of this book may be reproduced or utilized in any form or by any means, electronic or mechanical, including photocopying, recording, or by any information storage and retrieval systems, without permission in writing from the publisher.

ISBN-13: 978-0692238479 (IbbiLane Press)

ISBN-10: 0692238476

cover artwork by Alexis Lipson-Nomides

cover design by Denise Eggman

back cover photo by Susan Shepherd

To my amazing husband, Trek, who met me when I was broken, fell in love with me anyway and who has held on so tightly and loved me so completely that all my broken parts went back together and I became whole again.

And to our friend Barry; the world is so much darker without you in it.

Contents

Introduction	ix
Begin at the beginning	1
Find your personal truth	13
Examine your habits	23
Making peace with yourself	29
Embrace your uniqueness	47
Always be grateful	57
Release fear	63
Letting go of the past	77
Rebuilding, or building for the first time, Self-esteem	87
Are we really making ourselves sick?	103
Do I really have to learn how to meditate?	109
Using music in meditation	117
Learn to use visualization	121
Love and light?	129
What is spirituality anyway?	135

A very simple explanation of the Law of Attraction	141
You're going to have some bad days	151
Childhood Trauma	159
Recovering from the death of a loved one	165
Introduction to part two	175
Energy work	177
What about working with crystals?	189
Totem Animals	193
Plants as totems	201
Developing psychic abilities	205
Two Pebbles	213
Afterward	219

I started writing this book many, many years ago and simply did not finish it. I know the book I would have finished at that time would have been a very different book than this one, and so maybe, "that" book was not really the one I was supposed to write. At least, that's my take on it.

For many years, I would think about writing and then talk myself out of it. A combination of a fear of failure as well as a fear of success kept me putting it off until the shocking untimely death of a very close friend reminded me that we do not always have as much time to do things as we think we do. So, the book you are now reading was completed.

It is my hope you will enjoy this book, find something useful to your path within these pages and ultimately be inspired to go out and make your light shine a bit brighter than before. If you have walked a path similar to my own, I hope you recognize within this book the fact you can do anything and be anyone you choose - no matter what anyone, including your own subconscious mind, has to say.

Thank you for reading, and I would love to hear from you!

Begin at the beginning

What do you see? Look around you right now and notice, what are your surroundings like? Take it all in. What do you see? If you are sitting inside, are you noticing what needs cleaning, are you seeing the clutter that needs to be put away, or do you see the lamp you picked out at the store with your best friend or the plaster handprint your child made in school when they were small?

If you are outside, are you noticing the plants that need to be trimmed and the grass that needs to be mowed, or how the house sure could use a new coat of paint, or are you seeing the tree that has sure grown a lot since you planted it with your dad, or the flowers you planted with your spouse that one really wonderful Sunday afternoon?

Take a moment to really think about what you really see. Of course, there are always things that we need to do, like clean the house and trim the bushes, but often we get so caught up in doing things that we forget to really see things. How you perceive your world has a direct line right into your heart and soul.

If you've been going through a really rough time, maybe you need to think about what you're seeing in your life, and more importantly, what you are not seeing. It is my hope that through this book you will be able to see things a bit brighter than before.

If you have been drawn to this book, it's a good chance you've not always had the type of life you would have preferred. Perhaps, you've even been depressed, overly stressed and/or abused at one time or another. Perhaps you've suffered tremendous loss; maybe you've even suffered the loss of the love of your life.

No matter what brought you to the point along your path where you are currently residing, there's probably something you've always felt was missing. Some unseen "thing" you knew would make the difference in how you've experienced your life.

At times you felt you deserved a much better life and could even almost catch a glimpse of "what could be" in your mind's eye. But, those familiar feelings of inadequacy, guilt, doubt and self-loathing would come back around again and keep you from believing you could be or have anything more. Those feelings were, and are, all completely wrong.

Let me state, first off and right away, I am not a professional counselor nor am I a psychologist, psychiatrist or any other medical professional. I'm not qualified, nor do I intend, to give any medical or psychological diagnosis or prescribe any such treatments.

I'm simply someone who has successfully fought their own battles, vanquished their own demons and slayed their own dragons. Basically, I've started and stopped, backed up and started again many times along my journey through life and have come to realize I am really not all that different from anyone else who has encountered a less-than-idyllic pathway before them. Today I work as a Life Coach, helping others learn how to slay dragons of their own and move forward along their own paths as successfully, lovingly and peacefully as possible.

For a very long time in my life, actually about 20 years, I went from one illness, injury or disease to another. After a while it almost became a joke, people would say 'gee what's this month's problem?' While my lifestyle during this time was not nearly as healthy as it probably should have been, there really wasn't anything that unhealthy that could be blamed for my continued health issues. Doctor after doctor prescribed various medications, I underwent several surgeries, changed my diet, got better for a while, and then all-of-a-sudden I would be sick again.

I became sick and tired of being sick and tired and even seriously contemplated suicide at one time. Because of this my doctor sent me to a psychiatrist his obvious diagnosis being that I was depressed and suffering from anxiety because I was sick all the time. This was when I suddenly realized none of them, the doctors, pharmacists, counselors or even this psychiatrist was really trying to make me well. They were just treating symptoms in a half-hearted effort to make me feel better. What I wanted was to feel well. I didn't want to continue living from "pill to pill" which is what I felt my life had become.

Having put all of this behind me, I now refer to this time in my life as my "habitual illness phase." Sometimes we tend to be very stubborn about learning lessons along our path, and I'm here to tell you that illness can be a very persuasive teacher.

Through dealing with various illnesses, I learned I had to figure out how to take care of myself better, I learned I had to be patient and compassionate about others as well as myself and most importantly, I learned the power of meditating, exercising and energy work.

I learned I had to forgive myself and everyone else who had ever hurt me and I learned I had to learn how to let go of those negative events, memories, thoughts and emotions I had been so forcefully hanging on to.

My habitual illness phase actually came to an almost-abrupt end when I started actively working with energy healing, actually dealing with and letting go of the past and began embracing my latent spirituality. Folks the mind is an amazing thing; it's the most powerful tool known to man.

I do not mean to sound as if the clouds parted, a lightning bolt crashed down and I was healed, but once I honestly started the process of healing my mind and my spirit, and quite literally taking out the trash from my subconscious, healing my health and body seemed almost like a side-effect. This wasn't easy, in fact it is the most difficult thing I've ever done, but I will tell you the results are amazing!

Never stop growing, never stop trying and never stop learning, especially about yourself.

Probably the most important thing I've learned along my journey is to pay attention to the words you are using. The old saying "sticks and stones may break my bones but words can never hurt me" is just not true. Words have power. To this day any time I hear someone saying something negative either about themselves, or particularly when it's a parent talking to their child, my heart aches just a little bit.

If you hear something, negative or positive, about yourself over and over again you can't help but start to believe it. It can take many, many years to undo the damage caused by thoughtless, negative words. Some people are never able to undo this damage in their entire lives.

So, strive to make the words you say to yourself and everyone else, especially those you love, as positive and uplifting as possible. Your words really do become your thoughts and that really does have an impact on your health, your life and the lives of those around you.

If you want to play around with how words affect your mood try this experiment. You'll need to find a mirror, I normally use my bathroom mirror, but any mirror will work fine. First off, quiet your mind and take a couple deep breaths. Next look right into your eyes and say "you're great." Really put some feeling behind your words. Did you feel it? If you do this correctly, and I realize it might take a few attempts to do it well, you will actually feel better.

I don't recommend anyone ever tell themselves anything negative, but if you want to try to get the opposite effect, do this exercise again, only telling yourself "you're horrible." Feel the difference? Since you would never want to leave yourself with that thought, please go back and tell yourself you're wonderful again now.

I've used this exercise with myself and with clients, varying the words depending on the situation and you can tailor this to just about anything. For example, if you have to make a presentation you are nervous about simply tell yourself you are a wonderful presenter. The possibilities are endless. This is pretty much how positive affirmations work and we'll go more into that later. For now, just make it a practice to say nice things to yourself each time you look into a mirror.

When my daughter was very young, as most parents, I tried my very best to make sure she had a very healthy sense of self-esteem, self love and an abundance of confidence in her ability to do anything at all that she ever wanted to do. For some reason, when she was very young, I decided that every time I heard her say the word "can't" I would stop her immediately and make her sing what she always called the "Rubber Tree Plant" song. If you've never heard of this song, it's actually called "High Hopes" and it's from a 1959 movie called "A Hole in the Head." I believe the most popular version of this song was actually sung by Frank Sinatra.

As much as she hated this song when she was a child, I can't tell you how proud I was when I heard her talking about this song to her young step-son. To be perfectly honest, I have used these lyrics to motivate myself as well through the years. Sometimes humor really does have more of a positive impact than we realize.

Now, if you are like most people who have gone through dark times in your life, once you begin to try and lift yourself up you're going to find it just is not as simple a process as maybe you've been lead to believe through various books, tapes and lectures. In my case, I read some books, studied, read some more books, listened to tapes and even started meditating. Still, I could not seem to break through the grey cloud I seemed to be encased in. Sure, things would go much better for a while.

Then one little thing would happen and I would once again descend into my dark hole. On one particular day this little thing was a hubcap. Yes, a hubcap on my car. I was making a turn and a hubcap literally flew off of one of the tires on my car and bounced across two lanes of traffic, eventually popping up the curb at a gas station and coming to a stop beside a gas pump.

Today, I would find this hysterically funny, yet on that particular day my emotional state was so very fragile I had completely lost my sense of humor. I ended up going home and crying for the rest of that day and into the night. Yes, all over a hubcap. I'm sure you can think of similar events that have happened in your own life. Sometimes, we just take ourselves way too seriously, especially when we're wounded.

Not long after this event it occurred to me that while I was saying all the right positive things to myself, I did not really believe those things to be true. It was as if my conscious mind and subconscious mind were having an argument. For some reason, none of the books or tapes on positive thinking I had been reading and listening to really seemed to have an explanation for this. It was as if I had somehow done something wrong, after all, these books and tapes said this would work for anyone.

Since I had begun meditating, which I will go into in a later chapter, I decided to try an experiment and hold my question "why can't I break through my dark cloud?" in my head while calming my mind. I did this for probably five to ten minutes each day for three or four days until I was struck with something I had not considered prior.

Very clearly in my mind I heard "you forgot to take out the trash." My first thought was, of course, that yes, I had taken the trash out that morning because it was garbage collection day. Then it occurred to me that maybe the trash in question was not in the can outside the garage; maybe this particular trash was actually referring to all the negative thoughts and self-destructive opinions I held in my subconscious mind.

All the positive things I had started doing simply did not "sink in" because there were so many negative thoughts and feelings taking up all the room. I know that is putting it very simply, but that is how I looked at it. So began my journey on my life's true path, my journey to love and light and my journey to writing this book.

When the same things keep happening to you over and over again in your life, it's time to ask yourself "what lesson am I supposed to be learning that I am choosing to ignore?" Even with the best of intent, you simply cannot move forward until you've accepted where, and who, you've been.

That doesn't mean you should constantly be thinking about your past, it only means that you need to fully learn what you need to learn from your past so that your past does not keep happening in your future. The reason for this book's title is that you can't really move forward with your life's purpose until you've "taken out the trash" you've accumulated thus far through negative thoughts you've been holding onto in your subconscious mind.

I'm here to say "I've been there, I feel your pain and you can do this." So, where do you start? While there are as many ways to start a journey as there are people, the simplest answer is "just start." Making the decision to simply start your journey is the very first, and most important, decision you can make at this time.

Someone once told me that anything at all can be accomplished if you just make a decision to work towards your goal for 15 minutes each and every day. I have to say, I wish I had heard that advice years earlier because it is true. Pick one small thing you can do to move forward in your life and on your path every day and just do that for 15 minutes. Of course, you can always continue past that 15 minutes, but we're really talking "baby steps" here so 15 minutes a day will be a terrific place to start.

As a writer, I found that making myself sit down and actually write for just 15 minutes was therapeutic as this small amount of time seemed to actually free up my thoughts so that I could let the words flow through me onto paper rather than over-thinking every word. It became sort of an "automatic writing" experience for me and much of what I wrote really didn't make sense at first glance. However, when I went back over what I'd written later on, I found some very insightful ideas that proved useful in my future writings and even with many of my life coaching clients.

Taking just 15 minutes at a time is a very useful technique for things like learning meditation or starting an exercise program as I also discovered. Actually, taking just about any task in 15-minute-increments is a very doable accomplishment and when you're starting out on your journey to the best "you" you can be, it is vitally important to build confidence and courage in yourself.

These very small accomplishments add up and give you the courage you need to take bigger steps. Taking bigger steps leads to you having more confidence and so on, until one day you realize just how very far you've come. You've got this. Really.

At the beginning of this new journey you've begun, don't be surprised when you find yourself becoming distant from certain people, places or things that used to be constantly in your life. This is simply because as you grow in your spirituality, you naturally gravitate towards those things that will assist you in moving forward on your path and away from those things that no longer resonate with who you are becoming.

This doesn't mean you have to completely stop going places or seeing people you've been around forever. It simply means you will probably notice you no longer feel like doing so as much as in the past. While it's certainly understandable and even perhaps commendable to talk to your friends and family about your new path, don't feel badly when they won't want to walk it with you.

And, most certainly, don't let their negativity about it make you quit your journey before you even really get started. Most often I recommend people just beginning on a spiritual path not be overly sharing when it comes to their awakening, especially when they are still brand new to it. Give yourself some time to figure things out for yourself, then when you are comfortable in your direction feel free to share all you'd like.

Find your personal truth

Each one of us is on their own unique path, no one's path has a judgment attached to it, and it is simply a path. Very small children understand this and if you've ever spent time watching pre-school children playing most often you will see many different activities going on at the same time.

You might have a group of kids running around playing some sort of an active game; you'd probably see a group of kids playing around or on a swing-set, monkey bars or on a slide. Of course, there would also be the loners, those one or two kids off by themselves doing whatever they wanted. There would probably be kids doing all sorts of things not worrying in the least about what anyone else thinks about what they're doing.

It isn't until an adult comes along and points out their differences that these kids will think they're doing something wrong. Children have to learn to see the differences between us; they have to be taught that these differences are wrong.

What were you like as a young child? Do you remember? Many of us can't really remember what it was like to be that young and feel that free. Some of us have spent years trying to pry those memories from the dark recesses of our mind so that we can remember. Unfortunately, many people have very dark memories from that early childhood time period.

Whatever your childhood was like it's time to let go of the unpleasant memories and emotions associated with them and reclaim a bit of the unbridled exuberance of simply being a very young human being. As I've said before, I've been informed it's really never too late to have a happy childhood and it's perfectly acceptable and even preferable, to let go of the bad stuff you remember and remember something really great to replace it.

What did you want to be when you grew up? Of course most of us had many images of what we could be and do when we became adults, because our lives were a blank canvas at that time. We could literally do or become anything. So, what was your grandest dream for your future? In my case, I wanted to become a veterinarian. When I was very young, all of my best friends were animals...the real kind, not only the stuffed variety.

For one reason or another every spring baby birds ended up in our house where we would hand-feed them in our attempt to save their lives. I had a wonderful grandmother and when I was quite young my mother was happy and I remember them carefully trying to coax these baby birds into eating. I remember my mother doing the same thing with kittens and what turned out to be a particularly long-lived chihuahua when he was just a tiny puppy. I even had a pet rooster as a child.

Because of all of these things most of my happiest times as a child involved animals. I didn't realize it at the time, but I received an amazing education in life and love very early in my life that would stay with me always. Unfortunately, a part of this lesson taught me to trust and love animals because they were always there for me...people on the other hand, maybe not so much. This was a part of the lesson I hadn't even realized I had learned until much later in my life; and then it took quite a while to un-learn it and give people a chance.

See, my biological father was not present. This was a time period when illegitimate children were looked down on and truly not accepted. Through my mother's actions and from overhearing comments from various people, I felt like I was not good enough, I learned that people couldn't be counted on to stick around and I thought I was "bad."

My mother was in so much pain from how she felt that the two of us were being perceived that she made it her goal to find a father for me and while I loved my "new" father, things were not really all that great at home. Both he, and my mother, very much wanted "things," they always talked about how everything would be perfect if they only had more money.

However, they spent money they really couldn't afford to spend and their family grew and grew to eventually include eight children. Neither one of them had received much of an education, and while they were hard-workers when they had jobs, there was a long period of time when neither one of them seemed to be capable of holding a job for very long. I grew up feeling confident in the fact that if it had not been for my saintly grandmother we would surely have starved to death.

As my siblings grew older, and as more siblings came into the world, the sense of fear and anger was palpable. The very few friends I had made in school no longer wanted to come to my house because my house "didn't feel good" to be in anymore. I'm quite sure today that neither of my parents realized what they were doing, I simply can't believe they would have set out to do such a thing intentionally, but our house was not usually a very happy place.

Add to this the beginning of physical confrontations between siblings and between parent and child. Suffice it to say it was not a calm and pleasant place full of love and light.

Eventually my mother became so overwhelmed she simply stopped trying to intervene in sibling fights, and the younger of my siblings today report they pretty much raised themselves. My father became so overwhelmed he found a simple job he learned to love and worked up to 18 hours per day. While at the time people were saying what an awesome guy he was working so very hard to feed his family, he admitted to me once that he really worked so many hours so he wouldn't have to go home.

Of course, by this time I was an adult with my own problems dealing with a young child and an abusive husband and simply told him I understood completely; which I most certainly did, I would not have wanted to be there either. I don't mean to sound as if everything was doom and gloom with my childhood family; while certainly this was a dysfunctional family I do have many memories filled with laughter and downright silliness.

The one thing I couldn't ever understand was how did two people so seemingly focused on having money, go so very far in the opposite direction? It occurred to me that maybe they weren't the only people to have done this and so I started reading every book I could get my hands on about how some people are successful while others are not.

However, just as I thought I was onto something, the abusive situation at my own house escalated and I was shoved right back down into relative ignorance about how life should be. This cycle would continue for me many more years.

If you've recognized any part of yourself in my story, I want first to reassure you that you and I are not the only ones this story sounds familiar to. There are many of us who have survived such a childhood and it's no wonder, to me, why there are so many dysfunctional adults wandering around today.

But, somewhere within your own personal story are the seeds of greatness for your future. Somewhere here is one particular moment you can remember when you realized this was not what life was all about. You caught a glimpse of what your life could be; you just couldn't understand how on earth you would get from here to there.

Somewhere along my path I came to a realization that within your earliest childhood dreams of what you wanted to be when you grew up was your truth. That thing you were sent to earth to do, that thing your soul knows you are supposed to be. Whether you wanted to be a veterinarian like myself, a fireman, a super-hero or a doctor; truly, you want to take care of others. It is your destiny to be a loving, kind and compassionate being who finds great joy and even gratitude in being able to be helpful to other beings.

So, you wanted to be a teacher instead? Or an astronaut? How about a paleontologist or archeologist? If you find yourself in these choices, you most likely were sent here to explore and find the answers, then teach them to the rest of us. If you didn't find your childhood dream in these examples, dig deep into your subconscious mind and listen to what it tells you.

Find whatever your truth is and start walking on your true path. Simply rediscovering your truth could very well be the most rewarding thing you will ever do for yourself.

Somewhere along the way most of us lose our truth. We get caught up, like my parents did, with trying to accumulate things, or money or whatever it was or is, and we lose sight of our original goals and dreams. We become shadows of what we should become and we don't even realize it is happening until it is seemingly too late to stop it. But it is never too late. You can go back and pick up the pieces of your dreams and start again. No matter how old you are. Age is just a number. How many times have you seen a story about a 90-something-year-old person who had just received their high school diploma or college degree? Find your truth and walk that truth, no matter what anyone else says about it...even if that "anyone else" is your own subconscious mind.

Right now, someone reading this is saying "ok, but I really do want money." There's nothing wrong with that, but you must be honest about it. Is it the actual money you want, or is it whatever you would do with money that is really what you want? Is it perhaps something you might buy with the money? Might there be another way of doing whatever it is, or having whatever you want, without having the actual money? Let's say, your dream is to own your own business.

Obviously, you're thinking "well to own a business you have to have money". Wrong. Many people have started businesses without a dime to their name, myself included. Yes, it would have been easier with money, but it can be done without it. You just have to decide to start, and you have to be open to accepting those opportunities that will inevitably present themselves to you once you have truly made your decision.

Stories abound about successful landscapers who started their companies with a borrowed lawnmower, musicians who lived in their rehearsal studios and computer programmers who originally worked with borrowed computers. Pick an industry and you will find a corresponding story. When it comes right down to it, the only thing truly in your way, is you.

What if you want a car? You certainly have to have money to buy a car, right? What if you don't really need to buy a car? I can tell you from personal experience it is possible to own a car without having money to buy it. Everyone has a special skill or talent, even if you haven't discovered yours yet. Do not discount the possibility that there is someone with a car they don't need who might very well need your particular skill. One time I actually bartered tiling someone's bathroom in exchange for a car they'd had sitting in their garage for years. I know others who have had similar experiences.

You just have to keep your eyes open and be willing to take action on those opportunities the universe puts in your path. So very often, instead of seeing the opportunity, we see the roadblock in front of us and struggle as we find a way to walk around it.

Remember the exercise from the very beginning of the book about seeing things? Learn to see things in a different light and you'll find your truth, and the path will become clear.

Once you do find your own truth, it will resonate so deeply within you that you can't "not" move forward on that path. It will grab you and hold on so tightly that while you might stumble on your way, you know without a doubt that you will get there. You just keep trying over and over again.

Even when it seems like you've "failed" you just keep getting right back up and starting again. Understand you will most certainly fall from time to time. Many people make the mistake of saying "well it just wasn't meant to be" and they quit.

Maybe whatever that was simply wasn't supposed to be your vehicle for success, maybe you need to be open to seeing a different method. And, while it is important to learn to trust your gut and recognize that if you're contemplating doing something that leaves a pit in your gut this is something you should not do; it is also important to learn the difference between that pit in your stomach and the fear that we often feel when we're on the right path but we need to move past our comfort zone.

Let me tell you something, sometimes the universe is just trying to show you a better way to achieve the same ultimate goal. Sometimes we perceive failure when really it's a misunderstood success. Try again, and again and again and again if necessary. Eventually you will get there.

Many of those who have walked very difficult paths and have succeeded believe that any time you run into a very difficult time period in your life, it means you are really one step closer to breaking through and achieving your goals. Don't you dare give up just when you're about to succeed!

Remember that saying that it's always darkest before the dawn? Turns out, that's a true statement in more ways than one.

Examine your habits

We all have habits, and not all of them are bad. Many if not most are actually good habits. What's the first thing you do after getting out of bed in the morning? Brush your teeth? Brush your hair? Shower? If you've been on a self-improvement path recently, you might even meditate, or do some form of exercise. These are all things that enhance our lives and keep us healthy.

But, not everything we do habitually is good for us. Let's look at breakfast. What? You don't eat breakfast? Do you realize that even something you don't do is a habit? You have a habit of not eating breakfast. Or, do you grab a quick cup of coffee and pastry for breakfast? Again, this is a habit, and not a really good one.

Many people with self-esteem issues fall into these habits and acknowledging these habits exist is the first step in changing them into habits that are better for us. A huge part of progressing along a spiritual path is taking care of your body. You really can't feel your best emotionally or mentally if your body isn't functioning as well as it can.

Other habits are a bit harder to see and maybe those more hidden habits are the most damaging to our lives. For example, if someone keeps hurting you and instead of changing your situation you simply add the latest hurt to the pile of hurts already in your heart and soul. You've created a habit of allowing yourself to bury your trash. You probably don't see it that way, but it's the truth. Eventually, in order to repair your heart and soul, you're going to have to change this habit.

Change is difficult. Changing your living situation or leaving a relationship you've already put "your everything" into is even more so. But, you absolutely must change if you've established the bad habit of allowing yourself to be hurt time and time again. Especially if you keep allowing the same person to hurt you every time. And, keep in mind, this doesn't have to be a physical "hurt", emotional scars are often much more difficult to move past.

Start with admitting this is actually happening. Realize it completely. Allow yourself to feel whatever emotions come up when you're doing this. If you feel anger, shame, frustration...whatever you feel is exactly the right emotion for you to feel at this time.

Accepting that you have allowed this situation to continue and that you are no longer going to allow it is the next step. You absolutely must be firm with yourself on this one. You have to find enough love and respect for yourself to stand up for yourself and not allow someone to hurt you anymore. This is much more difficult than it sounds to a lot of people.

Forgive yourself for allowing someone else to have so much power over you that they were able to hurt you again and again. Forgive the person who hurt you for being so weak they had to try and make themselves feel better by hurting you. Sit down and write yourself a note detailing everything you want to change and then work to change those things.

Understand that unless you truly handle your own mental and emotional habits, whatever happened in this relationship will happen again and again.

Know that you can now establish a good habit to replace the bad one you're trying to get rid of. This will take some work, but knowing what you need to do really is the worst part. None of us want to admit we're at least partially to blame for a bad relationship or a friendship-gone-wrong and you might find you feel you're fighting with yourself as you try to change those bad habits within yourself.

Although it will take a lot of determination and work, you will be able to do this. And, you must do this for yourself and your bright future and happy life that you deserve. You'll have to be vigilant and really pay attention to how you act and what you say and whether or not you are still internalizing things as you progress to other relationships.

When you catch yourself slipping back into old habits, simply notice it and correct it right away. Take the time to write down these times as you notice them and you'll begin to get a picture of when you are most susceptible to back-sliding into old habits.

If you find yourself internalizing things when you are really tired and just don't think you have the energy to deal with whatever it is at that time, you'll learn you need to at least bring it up and then tell the other person that this is something that hurt you but you're really too tired to talk about it right now and make the decision to talk about it after you've rested.

Or, if you feel the other person wouldn't let the conversation go until another time, simply write it down for yourself and revisit it with this person later. Make sure you're doing so in a calm manner and make sure the other person knows you're just making them aware of something that is an issue for you and you're not trying to fight.

If this person insists on an argument instead of a conversation, it might really be best for you to just walk away and not pursue a relationship with this person. Choosing the same type of person to start a relationship with over and over again is also a really bad habit!

Don't forget to replace the old habits with new ones as you go along. For example, let's say you find yourself with a friend who just never seems to have time for you and/or makes plans with you then flakes at the last minute; yet, you still keep trying to make plans with this person. The next time you feel the urge to make plans with this so-called friend stop yourself and do something different. Stop allowing yourself to be hurt by people who have proven they don't really care about you. Find someone else to go out with, or go to a movie by yourself. Or just get outside and go for a walk.

Negative self-talk, being overly critical of yourself and not seeing what a wonderfully unique and special person you are can also be considered bad habits. As you progress along your new life's path, you will want to pay special attention to these areas so you are able to identify what specific bad habits you have developed regarding how you see and talk to yourself. This way, you'll be able to work to get these bad habits out and new and good habits in. Again, this is a process and it will not be an easy one, but you will prevail.

Inevitably you will find there will be times you'll slip back into old bad habits. Don't be too hard on yourself as change is very difficult. Just notice it, and start again. Stay determined to persevere and you will certainly be successful. Everyone has bad days...the successful ones realize it's only a day and doesn't mean their whole life is a failure. I've said it before and I will say it again; you can do this.

Making peace with yourself

Have you heard the phrase "make peace with it?" Most often people say this when they've been hurt, or done something they're ashamed of, or they've had a fight with someone they love. Usually this is just another way of saying to "let it go."

But, really, I do believe it is possible to let something go and not really be completely at peace with yourself about the situation. You might really have forgiven whoever else was involved, and maybe you've even forgiven your own part in whatever transpired, but from time to time you still feel like you've never really accepted the situation. You still keep reliving it over and over again in your head. Obviously, if you're doing this, you are not really at peace with it.

Before you can truly make peace with the world at large, people in general or even that one person you've had a dispute with, you must first make peace with yourself. While this probably sounds like an obvious statement to you, think about what it really means.

Too often we try to "make" the other guy apologize before we forgive them, or we want to "force" someone else to make amends for some error in judgment when we might have actually fed into their views. As you most likely already know, these attempts to make someone else do something will only lead to a disappointing result.

You just can't make anyone else do, or feel, anything. At best, you will only receive "lip service" which truly means nothing at all. In any case and whatever the circumstance, we need to realize that being at peace really starts, and ends, with us, ourselves.

There is an old saying, to love someone else you first need to love yourself. I do not know if there is a saying, to forgive someone else you first need to forgive yourself or not, but there should be if there isn't. So many people go through their lives holding on to mistakes they've made or fights they've had or even things they should have done but never quite got around to doing.

If this sounds familiar to you, then stop right now and say to yourself, "I forgive me." We are all human, and as such, we are not even close to being perfect. Everyone makes mistakes, everyone does stupid things from time to time and we have all done things we can't imagine how we ever thought were good ideas of things to do. It's ok. Really, it is.

Early on in my adult life, and very soon after my abusive marriage ended, I was in a relationship that really went from a very loving and positive one to one that truthfully should have ended years before it finally did. Probably because of our youth and inexperience with what a good and lasting relationship should be, we never discussed anything that either of us felt and completely stopped trying to find things to do together. We simply grew apart. So, we got to a point where we were living separate lives except for those infrequent times we'd both be home at the same time.

You would think we would have enjoyed each other's company since we were, after all, in a relationship. But, instead of enjoying our time together we always seemed to end up fighting. We weren't physically fighting, but we certainly knew how to push each other's buttons, and as almost anyone can attest, sometimes these mental and emotional fights end up causing the most damage.

By the last year we were together we had entered into a very unhealthy sort of 'you hurt me so I'll hurt you' contest that today seems laughable and I really don't recognize either one of us as we are today in that earlier time. In any case, this very negative relationship dragged on way longer than it should have and finally one day I went home and my "insignificant other" had simply packed up and moved out while I was at work.

To add insult to injury, almost immediately after this happened my best friend decided to choose drugs over our friendship and she was gone as well. Just about a month after both of these people were out of my life, my saintly grandmother died. It was just way too much for me to handle at that time in my life. Talk about a trial by fire. This is undoubtedly the darkest time period in my life.

The overwhelming and quite unexpected anger I felt over the, at the time, newly ex-boyfriend was both extreme and extremely unhealthy, and for years after this happened I could not accept that I'd played any part in that relationship's ultimate demise whatsoever. I truly was blinded by rage.

I would have expected to feel hurt and possibly even betrayed, and to a point I did. But what I felt mostly was pure unadulterated anger. I was angry at him for moving out when I was at work instead of telling me this was going to happen, I was angry at him for leaving at a point during the month when there was no way I could come up with the entire rent, I was angry at him for taking the dog with him. Of course, I was also hurt. But what really took me by surprise was the depth of the anger I felt.

It really wasn't until after I'd had a chance to calm down and put several years between myself and that event that I came to realize I had been just as guilty a party to our very destructive relationship as he had been, and it truly was a very good thing we were no longer together. Then it still took me a long while to completely process what had really happened and how much I needed to let it all go so I could move forward with my life.

But, I finally did get to that point, we both did, and once that happened and we both sincerely forgave each other and ourselves, and we were able to look back and see that we really did have some good times in there as well. We made peace with each other and with ourselves.

The best friend who had chosen drugs above our friendship, and truly did this at the time I most needed a best friend, eventually came around and got clean and sober. While it took us a very long time, we did eventually become friends again, and remain friends to this day. Although, truthfully, we are not nearly as close as we once were, and I sincerely hope that one day we might find our way back to that level of trust that best friends have.

Again, though, I came to realize that I wasn't as good a friend to her as I should have been either. Maybe if I had paid more attention to what was going on in her head I would have realized she was developing a habit and I could have intervened before it truly became a life-threatening problem. One lesson inherent in both of these situations is that no one is ever completely innocent in a situation. We all play our parts in all of our relationships and sometimes those parts we play aren't very pretty.

The death of my grandmother is something I will go into a bit later in this book, but suffice it to say I still miss her to this day and know for a fact I would never have been able to accomplish anything positive in my life at all without her in my corner. She truly was an amazing woman who was light years ahead of her time.

Maybe you've been in a very abusive relationship, or you've been involved with someone who has had an addiction of some kind or other. Maybe you, yourself, have been the abuser or has suffered from an addiction. If any of these things ring true to you in your past relationships, you've probably had the horrible fights that usually ended with the "I'll never do (whatever it was) again." And, because you desperately wanted to believe this person, maybe you've believed it when you said it yourself, you just couldn't walk away.

In any event, you continued the relationship and sure enough, the situation would happen all over again within a short period of time. This is a very common merry-go-round that isn't "merry" at all. It takes a great deal of strength to break out of these situations and often, when we do eventually get out, we spend the next months, years or even decades beating ourselves up because we didn't get out, or get help, sooner. Again, it's ok. It's in your past and you were coping the best way you knew how to cope at the time.

Forgive yourself for allowing that situation to continue and forgive the other person for being the way they were at that time. Forgive yourself for being weak, scared, scarred, self-centered, selfish...whatever you feel you were at that time. It is in the past and nothing you can do, say or feel about that situation can ever take it back or change it at this point in your life. You don't have to forgive everything anyone did, just forgive the person, with as much love and peace in your heart as you can muster.

You also have to understand that we each have our own points of view and just because you see a certain situation in one light doesn't mean the other party sees things the exact same way. This doesn't mean someone is "right" and the other is "wrong" it just means you are different people. Agree to disagree, and really and truly do it, and then, put it behind you.

Many times people have said to me that they just don't believe it's important to them to be able to forgive someone else when that person is not in their lives anymore. Often they say they don't even know where the person is or how to contact them. This is not important.

What we're trying to achieve is for you to come to terms with whatever you've gone through to the point where you can let it go and not have it constantly creeping back up to hold you back from the beautiful future you deserve.

Simply because, I personally, do not believe you can really come to terms with the past without forgiving it, I strongly advise people to work on this. As I've said before though, you really can't make anyone do anything, so if you feel strongly that you are able to let go of the past while not forgiving any of it...that's your choice, it is, after all, your path.

A part of making peace with yourself is being completely honest with yourself. You are not perfect and never will be. When someone else makes you angry, you have to be honest with yourself and recognize that just like you can't make someone else apologize and mean it, no one else but you can make you angry. People can do things that will bring out the anger you are already harboring inside yourself, but they do not put the anger there, you already had it.

The same thing goes with any emotion, people cannot make you feel anything...you are allowing yourself to be so completely influenced by others that you are allowing them to tell you how to feel. Stop it. Forgive yourself for allowing this to happen and understand that you always have a choice in what emotion you want to experience.

Don't give anyone else so much power over you that you become like a tattered flag blowing in the wind of their whims. Take your power back and keep it for yourself. Sometimes we get to the point where we can move on from one person we've allowed to take control of our lives, but then we move right onto the next person who we allow to do the same thing. You absolutely must get to the point where you do not allow anyone to ever have so much influence over you that you lose yourself.

At one time in my life I had a friend who was always angry, always in pain and always very unhappy with the world in general. Yet I could see a very wonderful person underneath this very dark exterior, so I thought I wanted this person in my life. For a very long time I felt as though I should "fix" this other person and I did everything I could think of to make this person happier.

It took months before I realized that instead of making them happier, I had become very unhappy. After a while I started finding things in general just weren't working out for me when they had been only a short time prior. I had by this time come a long way on my path and was convinced I had the ability to help others.

Now, I know I was not ready for this at that time. I had not yet learned how to help someone else and not take on their issues as my own. The more time I spent with this person the worse I felt. Instead of me bringing them up, they were bringing me down.

During one morning's meditation, I became painfully aware of what I had been allowing to happen. First, I have to admit, I got angry at the other person for making me feel bad; then, I realized it was my own fault. Not everyone who comes into your life needs or wants your help with their path, they are on their own personal journey.

This was a very important lesson for me at that time, and it should be to you as well. It is fine to offer assistance if you feel you might be able to help someone else. Very often, we even end up helping ourselves more than we actually help the other person by doing this.

Just make sure you aren't dealing with an "energy vampire." You know those people who just seem to suck the very life out of anyone who spends any amount of time with them. If this happens to you, like it did to me, understand you are not the only person to find themselves in this situation and you should never feel bad for trying to help someone else.

You can love someone dearly and not have them in your life...you have to know when to let them go. In my case, I did feel bad for quite a while after cutting this person out of my life; almost as if I expected them to suddenly come to their senses and make great strides in personal growth therefore making it possible for me to have the friendship with them I had originally wanted.

Of course, that did not happen, and that's ok, their path simply was not congruent with my own. When you try to teach someone something you know and accept as a truth and they just do not grasp the concept of what you are trying to help them understand, it simply means they are not ready for that information at that time.

It is sort of like trying to teach trigonometry to a kindergarten class...they don't have the foundation necessary to really digest the information. This doesn't mean you shouldn't try, it just means you shouldn't feel like you've failed. At some point farther down their path this very thing you tried to convey will suddenly make sense to them.

One of the most common sources of guilt people carry around with them is the experience of losing a loved one right after they fought with the person, or should have gone to see them and didn't. This is one of the most truly gut-wrenching feelings of guilt you can experience, mostly because there is no way to ever make amends with who you perceive is the injured party.

Please, understand your loved one doesn't want you to carry this guilt and doesn't want you to feel bad about whatever happened. They understand you love them and they want you to forgive yourself for the situation, no matter what that situation entailed or how badly you, or they, acted during that time.

If you've experienced a great deal of trauma in your life there's a really good chance you have also been depressed. Perhaps even you've either tried to or thought about committing suicide as I once did. Please don't feel bad for the depth of your darkness during that time.

Depression is a very real thing and those who have never dealt with it will never know how very lucky they are. There is a misconception about those who try to kill themselves in that people think they're weak or they just want attention.

Truthfully, they just want their pain to stop and they believe, truly believe, at that moment that their loved ones will be much better off without them. If they are truly suffering from depression they aren't trying to get attention for the sake of getting attention, they are showing how horribly they are hurting and how very deep their despair is and how desperate they are for the pain to stop. They're showing how very much they feel those people in their lives deserve better than the broken depressed mess they feel they've become. It is very likely that in the mind of a suicidal individual they aren't trying to hurt anyone else, they truly believe they would only hurt people if they actually lived.

Sometimes, when feeling in the depths of despair, it isn't easy to focus on the good times you've experienced. Still, those great moments are always with you, even if you occasionally forget them. Sometimes, you just need to find that first one single moment in your memory that makes you smile to let all those other ones come to the surface. You absolutely must search for that moment, and search for it until you find it.

If you've been there, you are not alone. If you are there now, please know that there is help available to you and there are people who truly and honestly do care. Please get help and find these caring people. If you love someone who has gone to this depth of despair and has lived, thank you for being there for them during the time they needed you most.

If you've lost someone who committed suicide, please do not ever think it was your fault and thank you too for remembering them as the vibrant, loving being they once were. If your life has been impacted by suicide, no matter what your role was, please make peace with it. Feel it, acknowledge your pain and ask the universe or whatever higher power you believe in to take it away. This is a very tough emotional dagger to remove from your heart, but be patient with yourself and you will remove it.

Of course, there are those people who actually do stage suicide attempts for the sake of getting attention. In my opinion, these people have other issues besides depression, although they may very well also be depressed. If you know someone who has, or is, fighting this battle, please do everything you can do to see that they get the help they obviously need.

If you are someone fighting this battle, please get help. Do it for yourself, those you love and who love you and the people who will come into your life in the future that will love you and that you will love. Do not deprive yourself of a beautiful future. Get professional help, there is no shame in needing this.

I promise you that if you do this at some point in the future you will look back at all the wonderful memories and people you've accumulated from the time you thought you had nothing further to live for and you will be so very grateful that you found a way through your dark tunnel of despair and persevered. I can promise you this because it's been several decades since I first pleaded with a higher power to let me die simply so the pain would go away.

There are people who were orphaned as children, people who were adopted and also people who grew up with an absent parent, maybe one they never even met. Often these people grow into adults feeling unworthy of being loved; they blame themselves and think they're the reason this other person was not around.

Sometimes these feelings are adequately resolved and they learn it was solely the absent person's decision to leave and truly the child who was left behind had little to nothing at all to do with that decision. Other times, the child grows into an adult always trying to find the absent parent, thinking that if they could just meet this parent everything would be great.

Many times they learn this absent parent has already died and they end up feeling guilty for never being able to meet them at all. They actually go through a grieving process feeling a deep sense of loss for "what could have been."

In the case of someone who was orphaned and/or simply adopted as a child, there is also often a feeling of the loss of identity, of "who am I really?" that is difficult to resolve. Again, some of these children grow into adults constantly searching for the missing parent(s) and blaming themselves for whatever happened to cause the parent(s) to not be there.

In any case, there is a good chance if you were a child who was left behind you carry some form of guilt associated with this event in your life. Please understand this was not your fault and had nothing to do with you as a person.

Of course, not all children who went through this experience grow into slightly dysfunctional adults; in fact, most do not. It seems to depend on how the particular circumstance was treated, if it was discussed openly and honestly with reassurance that the child is very much loved and cared for and about the chances are very good this experience will not have a negative impact at all.

I was one such child who unfortunately did not have an open and honest family who communicated well. While I had always "known" I had a different biological father from my siblings, it was not until I was a teenager that my mother, very dramatically, told me "the truth."

Being a very sensitive child, the tears streaming down my mother's face when she finally confirmed what I had always known were enough for me to never ask any questions. After all, why would I want to hurt my mother? There just didn't seem to be a way for me to get my questions answered without hurting her, so I didn't ask them. That doesn't mean I didn't have them though, and this "missing part" of myself was always in the back of my mind.

By the time, decades later, I learned my biological father's name and actually got a phone number it was far too late to undo the damage. It was far too late for this man that I sort of looked like, but was otherwise a stranger, to make any difference at all in my life. So, like many of those in similar situations, I felt grief over what I had missed out on, and guilt for not being good enough that he couldn't help but be in my life. And, also like many others in the same or similar situations, it took me many years to fully process and eventually discard these negative emotions.

Guilt can be a very heavy burden to carry around. No matter what you've done or think you've done to hurt anyone else, you have to look at yourself as an imperfect being capable of doing really dumb things that you'd love to "undo" if you could. Then mentally, undo it. Sometimes the person you think you've hurt the most has already forgiven you, and they don't want you to continue beating yourself up on their behalf anyway.

I know someone who was so distraught over something they did very early in their life to a friend they simply punished themselves to an extreme. They turned their guilt over this event so inward it was literally making them sick, they became incapable of allowing anyone else to get close to them so they ended up extremely lonely.

Eventually they entered therapy to find out why they didn't have friends and through a combination of counseling sessions and hypnosis they figured out their issue with friendship had actually begun way back in childhood when they had tried to make the popular kids like them by making fun of a close friend that had always been there for them. They had felt so badly about doing this, they had not only lost a friend, they lost themselves as well.

When they finally got up the courage to track down this long-lost friend, they discovered this friend had understood, forgiven and felt nothing but love for them. They had already been forgiven for this deed years ago, and the "un-friended friend" was more than happy to forgive again and certainly didn't want to be the source of anyone's unhappiness and guilt over something that happened so long ago when they were both kids.

Love yourself enough to feel the pain of your guilt and what it's done to your self confidence, self-esteem and self love; then, forgive yourself for everything you've ever done that you wish you could take back. And, mentally take it back, let it go and move forward.

Remember too that if you've created a situation you later feel guilty for, there is a lesson in there somewhere. Find and learn that lesson, be grateful for that lesson, and become a better person for having had that experience. Many of my friends and clients have utilized the following words, feel free to use these, or write, say or do whatever else resonates with you to help you forgive yourself and move forward along your journey.

'I give thanks to everyone and everything, from every world and realm, for all I have, have ever had and will ever receive.

I forgive anyone who has ever hurt me, intentionally or accidentally, whether through thought, word or deed, so that they may find peace and love in their heart and soul

I apologize to anyone I have ever hurt, intentionally or accidentally, whether through thought, word or deed; that they may forgive me and I, too, may find peace and love in my heart and soul

I send warm, comforting energy to those I love and to those I cannot no matter who or what they are, did or will be or do

As these words are uttered may they ring true.'

You must understand that you are, above all, an imperfect human being and you will stumble and fall along your way. While it is true that you can never dream too big, it is also true you can't take steps that are too small when you're in recovery mode.

It really doesn't matter what you're recovering from, you will need to be patient and kind with yourself when you seem to be stuck and love yourself when you seem to go backwards. Sometimes we are only able to process pieces of lessons at a time; if you find you keep reliving something in your mind, it might mean you are still processing the information.

You may need to do this several times before you are truly able to make peace with yourself in relation to this particular situation. However long it takes you to do this is absolutely the right amount of time for you to do so.

You will know you've been successful when you can objectively remember events without any emotional involvement and completely without any judgment. In my case, as in the case of others I've spoken with through the years, you may find yourself taking three steps forward and then two steps backward from time to time. It's ok; this is still moving in the right direction.

Embrace your uniqueness

Throughout my lifetime, I've been accused of being silly. I've heard it so many times from so many people I've long since grown tired of hearing it and to this day any time my husband says "you're silly" my response is "no, I'm perfectly serious." Yes, I am. I'm perfectly serious about my silliness. To be honest I don't think I would have survived many of the situations I'm encountered throughout my life if it weren't for my sense of humor.

Most, if not all, of my darkest hours have come when I've temporarily lost my sense of humor. Many times I've found something funny about a situation most people would have only found despair in. One time that comes readily to mind was a particularly violent outrage from my ex-husband. He was furiously throwing things around and went to kick my puppy just as the puppy left a puddle on the floor.

Well, as you can imagine, the force of a grown man's foot winding up in a deliberate kicking motion on a wet floor resulted in said man slipping and falling into the very puddle that had caused the floor to be wet. All I could do was grab the puppy and my daughter and leave the house. In hysterics. By the time we returned, he had calmed down and forgotten about whatever the original cause of his outburst had been.

While he never found this incident the least bit funny, and simply because of his own coping mechanisms he probably will not even admit today that he remembers it, I still chuckle about it to this day, many decades later. It is most certainly true that having a sense of humor will absolutely save your sanity.

Whether people think you're funny, silly, intelligent, selfish, loving or whatever else people say about you, pay close attention to what they say. No matter how your friends and family, those people closest to you, describe you, even if you disagree with them, it is a very accurate description.

It's funny how differently we see ourselves than how others see us. If people see you drastically different from how you see yourself, you probably need to do some serious soul-searching and figure out why that is.

A very good way of doing this is to find a quiet space and just do a mental inventory. When you think about your life, what moments have meant the most to you? What moments have taken your breath away? Don't try to force it, just be still and quiet and let these special moments surface.

When you've been able to retrieve your special moments, take a couple of minutes and compare them. What do they all have in common? Were the same people or situations involved? Did each of these special memories involve something funny, touching, scary? Many times these memories will have several things in common, and that's fine, try to find "you" in these memories. How did you react, what did you say or do, was this the same in each of these memories?

Most likely you'll come up with something about yourself that agrees with whatever people have said about you. If people think you're always serious, you've probably shown this to be the case many times. If people find you emotional, well, again, you've probably revealed this about yourself over and over again. And, of course, if people think that you are, like me, silly or funny...most likely you laugh or make other's laugh when it seems like the last thing anyone wants to do.

If you think of yourself as someone who takes things very seriously, yet everyone around you thinks you're emotional, maybe you need to take a good long look at what you're doing to make people perceive you as something you don't think you are. Or, maybe you need to learn to be more honest and accepting with yourself about who you are. In any case, you are always free to decide to be different than you've been.

People can and do change and you are no exception. So, if you'd rather people think of you as serious, or intelligent or silly or however you want to be seen...start being that way.

I always knew I was different from other kids. Every teacher I ever had pointed out how different I was, friends' parents pointed out how different I was and even my family pointed out how different I was. Except they didn't use the word "different" they used words like "odd," "so very strange", and "weird."

Now, I understand how very special I was and I consider it a wonderful thing that I was so very different; but then, it just reinforced the thought in my head that I was not good enough, or bad, or not wanted. As I've said before, words have power and they do hurt. At any rate, yes, I was very different from most children, at least those that I knew. And I so desperately wanted to be just like everyone else and to fit in. I tried many times to become someone else, but each time I just could not seem to pull it off and I felt more and more like a failure in simply being human.

From a very early age, I realized I could see things others couldn't see and I could feel things that others were feeling. Often, I could hear what they were thinking too, which only compounded my feelings of inadequacy. It's very difficult knowing right up front when someone really doesn't like you even though they don't know you at all.

Many times people would ask me who I was talking to and I couldn't understand how they didn't already know, after all, obviously I was talking to the person next to me. It didn't matter to me if they were alive or not. After a while I learned to pay attention to who was around so I could avoid these confrontations.

It didn't really seem to matter how hard I tried to hide, there was always someone with a new way to tease me. There were several times when kids I had thought were my friends would pretend they could see what I was seeing, and then they would turn around and make fun of me for admitting what I could see.

To this day, every time I hear someone talking about their child's imaginary friend, I wonder if they might be simply not seeing what their child sees so very clearly.

Feeling what others were feeling proved to be more problematic and while today I realize I'm an empath, in childhood I only knew I could be happy one minute and then pass someone on the street or in a classroom at school and suddenly be sad, or angry, or whatever that particular person was feeling at the time.

When I was about 8 or 9 years old, my mother's cousin committed suicide. I never met this person, so this event probably shouldn't have had an effect on me at all. Still I remember very clearly feeling exactly all the shock, grief and sadness flowing from my mother's heart straight to mine like a long shimmering ribbon connected us. I was so upset my mother became very angry with me and demanded that I stop being upset because I had never even met this person.

At that moment I realized she had no idea what I went through on a daily basis and knew I had to figure out how to control this "gift" I had been born with. Eventually, I did learn how to build "internal walls" and to turn off this gift. Today, I can still turn it on when I want to, but I've learned that I don't need most of the time.

Animals were always hugely important to me, especially as a child when I had few friends from school. Since I was typically a loner it was not uncommon for a teacher to find me at the edge of the playground talking to a bird, or squirrel or whatever other animal was handy at the time.

If a stray dog, cat or other animal got hit by a car, I was usually somewhere in the vicinity to send it love and light so it could either recover or have a quick and painless transition to the other side. If someone was being unkind to an animal of any kind I was the one to stick up for the animal.

There were many times I saved snakes, lizards and tarantulas on my school playground from being tormented and possibly killed by classmates. As you might imagine, this did nothing at all to make me appear any less "different" and I got teased often for this.

It was not only animals I stuck up for however, I naturally gravitated to any other "outcast" and often got into arguments or even the occasional fight at school sticking up for the underdog, whether it was an animal or another kid that just didn't quite fit in. Usually it was when a disabled child was being teased, but it could have just as easily been anyone. I never really understood exactly why I felt I had to stick up for the underdog at all times, but I always did. Actually, I still do.

I've spoken to many people through the years who could see and hear ghosts, speak to animals and who stuck up for those considered outcasts, as children and as adults. There seems to be a recurring theme among us that we were the ones who always seemed to be older than our actual age, always seemed to know more than we should have, were intensely independent and more often than not, had a definite creative streak.

Most of our teachers would describe us as "different", "sensitive", and "shy" or "introverted." Ordinarily we didn't have many friends and we were quiet unless we really had something to say, then you had a difficult time getting us to shut up. As a whole, we always seemed to be very passionate about a great many things and to believe we could actually make a difference, no matter how difficult our lives had been in the past or even at present.

Unfortunately, many of us also suffered greatly in school at the hands of school bullies who found our kind and gentle nature easy targets. The fact we were usually alone made it easier still. If you are one of us, please know there are many, many like you who have gone through exactly or very nearly the same things you have.

For some reason we, as human beings, seem to want desperately to fit in and be one of the crowd. We don't want to stick out or be different from everyone else. I know I spent a tremendous amount of time and effort trying to copy others and be someone I wasn't just hoping I would fit in.

I'm guessing this goes back to the "safety in numbers" thing we all grew up with and probably goes back farther than that to the very beginning of human evolution when the one who was not with the crowd was eaten. How very unfortunate we can't celebrate our unique gifts and talents more, since we are all human beings.

Can you imagine how very boring this world would be if we were all exactly the same, if not one of us were any different at all from the others? This world needs the creative people, the geniuses, the planners, the warriors; the world needs each and every one of us or we simply would not be here.

This world needs you and your unique talents, whatever they might be. So, embrace that part of you that makes you the most different from anyone else; embrace your uniqueness.

There will always be bullies, there will always be those people who just can't seem to help themselves and have to make fun of others, and there will always be those people who just don't like anyone who is even slightly different from themselves. Don't let them keep you from being yourself.

When I think about all those years spent just trying to fit in and be "normal" instead of just being me, it sort of makes me a little sad, like I've wasted precious time. Then I remember, all those years and "failed experiments" spent trying to be someone I wasn't only showed me how to look at things from a perspective other than my own. Each and every one of these "experiments" has made me the person I now am. And, that is an awesome truth.

Always be grateful

While it is perfectly obvious that we should be grateful for all the wonderful things that come into our lives, it is equally important to be grateful for those not-so-wonderful things that have come into your life as well. It might take some time for you to see it, but everything, good and bad, that has happened in your life has conspired to make you into the person you are right now.

I know, you're thinking 'but some really terrible things have happened to me.' I understand. And, I'm telling you that these terrible things have contributed just as much to who you are as all those wonderful things you've gone through have. If nothing else, those bad events have made you stronger, simply because you have survived.

Most likely they've also made you wiser, because you have probably learned a lesson or two along the way. Perhaps some of these events have made you enjoy the good moments in your life a little bit more than you used to, because you are aware that not all moments will be good ones. Maybe you've learned to appreciate people and things a little bit more, because life can and often does, change in the blink of an eye.

If you are alive, and you are because you're reading this, you should be grateful. If you are getting older and experience pain more often than you used to, you should be grateful. So many people do not get the chance to get old, or even live to adulthood.

No matter what has happened to you or through you in your past, you should be very grateful that you survived to be here today. If you can see and hear, be grateful, because there are so many people who can't. If you can walk, run, dance...again, be grateful, because these are things so many of us can't do anymore and there are so many others who never could.

By being grateful for those things and those people you currently have in your life, you are telling the universe "yes, I want more of that." This is a big part of the Law of Attraction you've no doubt heard a lot about, and on which more will be written in another chapter.

By keeping yourself in a state of being grateful you will find you become more compassionate and loving in general. You will find little things that used to be extremely annoying are not nearly as annoying. You will find that things really do seem to start going your way.

Being grateful signifies you are happy with the way things are right now instead of constantly chasing whatever you think you are in need of. It keeps you focused on what you have instead of what you don't have.

When you think in these terms, it's easy to see how very lucky you already are in your life. It is easier to learn the lessons you need to learn in order to move forward in your life. And if you are truly grateful, whatever lessons present themselves will be easier to process and learn.

Being grateful is a lot like simply being positive, you will get back whatever you put out there. If you're grateful for what you've already got, you'll find yourself getting more of it; if you're positive, you start seeing positive people all around you. Basically, you will see whatever it is you expect to see, you can choose to see the good stuff or the bad stuff.

You can find really bad elements in most good things and you can find really good elements in most bad things. Whatever it is you find, be grateful for the experience, and remind yourself that you will indeed find whatever it is you expect to find in every experience you have. You can always choose to expect only the good stuff.

Every day, make it a point to wake up and be grateful you did wake up. Each day I thank the sun for rising, the house I woke up in, the dog that takes up most of my bed, even though she's really very small, and when I go outside I thank the birds for singing and the plants and trees for growing.

I have found this to be a very simple way of assuring I will have a beautiful day, no matter what happens. When you're really grateful, you can't really experience a "bad day" because by being grateful you are keeping yourself in an optimistic and positive mood.

One thing you should really try to see how this works, and how well it works, is the next time something happens that is not at all what you would have liked to have happened try being grateful for the experience. Here's just one example of how this might look.

Let's say you are sitting at a traffic light on your way home from work after having a really busy day. You just really want to go home and relax. Suddenly the car behind you slams into the back of your car. Great, right? That's just what you needed.

So, now you've had to call the police and your insurance agent, wait for a tow-truck; go through all the hassle of the time, effort and energy of dealing with a fender-bender.

Once you finally do get home and turn on the TV, you see news about a massive accident with fatalities that happened; only a couple of miles away from and a few minutes after your fender-bender. In fact, if you had not had the fender-bender, you probably would have been involved in that other, much more serious, accident. You might have even been killed.

Sound like an extreme example? Sure, it is an extreme example; but it happened to me. I became very well aware of how grateful we should be for whatever happens at the very moment I became aware of the accident people actually died in. All-of-a-sudden my 'really bad experience' became an 'ok, I can handle this' experience.

Now, of course, every fender-bender doesn't save you from a more serious accident. Of course, some really bad things do happen and it's extremely difficult to find anything at all about them to be grateful for. But, if you really concentrate on trying to be grateful for every experience I'm willing to bet you will start realizing that you're having a lot more positive ones popping up around you and a lot fewer of those bad ones. You'll also find yourself a whole lot happier in general and a whole lot better prepared to handle whatever comes your way.

I have found it very helpful when I'm feeling a bit down to sit and make a list of everything I am grateful for at that exact moment. If you do this, you might find it starts out very slowly and you can really only think of one or two things initially. Give it a few minutes. If you open your heart and mind just a second or two you'll realize that everything you have, everything you see, everyone you love is something to be grateful for. Just start writing, whatever pops into your head or whatever you see.

So, you've got a stack of clothing to go through and discard? Be grateful you have so many clothes you have to now give some away. Your car has a flat tire? Be grateful you have a car to buy tires for. You get the idea.

Strive for at least a full page of things you are grateful for, once you get started you'll probably have a much longer list. This exercise has never yet failed to improve neither my mood nor the moods of the numerous friends, family and clients I've suggested it to. Try it for yourself and you'll find this will improve your mood as well.

Release Fear

Release those things that make you most afraid and you will find true balance.

Be brave. I know that is a very vague phrase and means many different things to each of us; honestly, that is the point.

Everyone has something that frightens them, something they've really always wanted to do but were afraid to do it, something that maybe no one knows about but themselves. This can be as seemingly mundane as taking a walk by yourself or as adventurous as sky-diving. The "thing" itself isn't really important.

The important thing is to realize your fear is holding you back from doing something you really and truly do want to do. Please don't take this as a suggestion that everyone should immediately go out and do whatever they're most afraid of. If you're never really cared to go deep sea diving or sky diving, that's not something you should run out and do just because you find it frightening. But, there's something in all of us that we've secretly always thought about doing, something we've always been too afraid of actually doing to even mention to anyone else.

Do not trivialize your fears, thinking they're just something you've learned to live with and therefore are not important to living the future you want. Everyone has fear, you just have to learn how to not let your fear control your life.

Fear is a very powerful thing. Fear not only keeps us from doing those things we'd really love to be doing, fear of the unknown has kept many people in toxic relationships, and fear has even kept people from going to the doctor. Sometimes with absolutely disastrous results when an illness that could have been cured with earlier treatment ends up being fatal. Fear of success, fear of failure, I'm fairly certain there's a fear of just about everything. Human beings are just full of fear.

Fear keeps us from really living. You were put on this earth to live a happy, fulfilling and purposeful life and if you are full of fear that is just not going to happen. So, how do you get rid of fear?

First off, be honest with yourself. What is it that you are afraid of? Is this a real threat, or is it imaginary? For example, you might have a terribly unfounded fear of the color yellow. Most likely, unless you've been almost been almost killed by a yellow taxi cab or bus, this is an imaginary fear.

So, the question you need to ask yourself is "what is the likelihood that this fear will actually come to pass?" Then ask yourself, "What is the worst thing that could happen as a result?" If your fear has a real possibility of actually coming to pass and you realize that you will survive the worst possible outcome if it actually does happen, you should be able to let this fear melt away.

Even if you have a really, truly, legitimate fear as in a potentially dangerous work situation, thinking logically about how well-prepared you are for the situation; recognizing all the safety precautions that are in place and how infrequently accidents happen should help ease your fear.

If you still feel your fear is well-founded, you can either take some extra precautions to be safer, talk about your concerns to a co-worker or supervisor, or perhaps ultimately you can decide this is not the work situation you really need to be working in.

Most safety experts will tell you it's almost always the person who is completely paralyzed by their fear who ends up getting hurt on a hazardous job-site. Being prepared, staying vigilant, and being confident in both ability and the preparation for the task at hand are what work for most of those with dangerous jobs.

Of course, you can still get hurt even if you do not work in a hazardous job. Vigilance, really being present and paying attention to what you are doing is the best way to make sure you do not get injured.

Absolutely, accidents can and do happen all the time, but you can most certainly reduce the likelihood that you will be involved in one by paying attention and staying present in the moment. Plus, if you are paying 100 percent of your attention to what you are doing, you will find you don't even have time to experience fear. This works equally well through all aspects of your life. Many people go through life simply not paying attention or being present.

The uncomfortable fact is most fears are based on beliefs we falsely believe to be true. That is, they are imaginary beliefs based on negative programming from our past. Some of these negative programs are as simple as a parent telling you to constantly "be careful." While certainly your parents did not mean this in a negative way, your subconscious mind probably took this as 'the world is dangerous so I should be afraid of it.'

Many of our negative programs came to us from our early childhood education experiences. Do you remember being on a playground and having a teacher or another adult tell you not to climb the tree or fence because you could fall? How about not to run around a pool? Yes, these items were simply to protect us, to make sure we didn't get hurt.

However, these items may also have been stored subconsciously as "these things are dangerous" and as "you don't want to get hurt." Of course no one wants to get hurt, but if the fear of getting hurt becomes overwhelming then you're left with an abundance of fear about something that may or may not have ever happened. This means you're left with a life that's not nearly as full as it could be.

Other negative programming may be more difficult to handle, such as a teacher telling you that you were stupid, a bully saying you were ugly or weak or even someone you had a crush on saying you weren't good enough for them to go out with.

However these negative programs got into your subconscious mind, you need to remove them in order to move forward. A very powerful technique that worked for me was to first pay attention to when I was being inundated with fear, then I would mentally say "that's not true" and replace my negative thought or fear with something positive.

For example, for a long time I was afraid to speak in public. I was convinced the audience would turn on me and not only not be receptive to what I was saying but actually heckle me until I left the stage. Of course, this was not going to happen, but it was really holding me back from doing what I knew I would enjoy doing.

So, each time my subconscious mind would give me a negative thought, like "people won't like what you say" I would retort, "yes, they will love what I have to say because they signed up for my talk." After a while I began to hear the negative thoughts less and less until these irrational fears went away completely. This does not mean I do not still experience anxious moments or have fearful thoughts, it just means I am able to handle those times and turn my nervousness into a better "performance."

Most people do not have either a particularly dangerous job, nor do most people routinely speak to groups. However, there are many, many people who are simply afraid of, well, life in general. Throughout my life there have been many times when I was one of those people.

If you find yourself being in this situation at this time in your life, please remember there are times in everyone's life when they experience fear in one form or another and everyone has had to overcome this fear themselves. Generally speaking, the overwhelming majority of people want other people to do well in life and to be happy, this includes you.

I know this sounds like a very simple thought, but once I decided to believe, really believe, this was true, I found myself experiencing less and less fear. You may find developing your own personal "mantra" that you repeat to yourself several times each day helps you as well.

Many of my clients have used this successfully. The key is to choose a phrase that resonates with you personally; one suggestion might be "I am confident and fearless." Whatever phrase you choose, make certain it is in the present and not the future and make sure it is positive and not negative.

For example, the phrase "I am confident and fearless" is a much better choice than "I will be confident and do not have fear." There are many places you can locate affirmations that are appropriately phrased; personally, I have found the most successful affirmations are the ones I make up for myself. We will go into affirmations and visualizations in a later chapter in this book.

One thing I've always found fascinating is people who have a fear of telling their significant other something. I've seen this time and time again through my life coaching clients. I've had people come to me and they can't figure out why they aren't as happy as they'd like to be or they can't figure out why their significant other isn't as happy as they should be.

Yet, upon talking for a while it will always be revealed that someone in the relationship is holding something back from the other party. It's amazing how often I find this. If you are in a committed relationship with someone you really believe you will spend the rest of your life with, why on earth would you be afraid to talk to them?

These are not terribly young, inexperienced people, these are people who are otherwise very intelligent, well-rounded individuals, many of whom hold important positions in their career or run their own companies. You would think conversations would not be a problem for them. Yet, even they find themselves afraid of confrontation or of having an unpleasant conversation.

In these cases I usually go through the usual "what's the worst thing you think would happen if you said..." Most of the time, a very deep fear of being alone or of being wrong or of hurting someone they really love or of not being good enough surfaces; yes, even in some of the most accomplished people I've ever met.

So you see everyone experiences fear, what matters is how you deal with it. Very often my life coaching clients are able to move forward once they realize the source of the fear; they just feel it, recognize it for what it is and decide to have their difficult conversation or plan out their confrontation anyway.

Many people have a very deep-seated fear of their past coming back to haunt them. This seems to be particularly true for those who have done something they've either been jailed for or should have been jailed for doing. It simply is not my "job" to judge anyone else, and really if the 'debt to society' was paid, what does it matter who did what way back when anyway?

At one time years ago I was in charge of deciding what job applicant to hire for a given position the company I had been working for had open. Among the stack of applications was one from a qualified individual who had only recently been paroled from prison. Since the person was qualified, I simply called him in for an interview along with the other qualified applicants.

When he arrived I was struck by how very insecure he seemed and I tried to calm him down by offering something to drink and asking him to please make himself comfortable. As the interview progressed I finally got to the point where I asked him flat out exactly what it was he seemed so frightened of. He said this was the seventh interview he had gone on since his parole and each one seemed to be less promising than the last.

He said that he was terrified of saying the wrong thing, so decided he would say as little as possible so maybe someone would decide he was worth taking a chance on. He confessed he felt every interview he had gone on was futile because people simply wouldn't give him a chance to prove himself.

This so touched me that I decided to hire him and give him a chance. He turned out to be one of the best employees I had ever hired. Still, many of his co-workers had decided he wasn't worth including in lunches and breaks that they would all get together on.

No matter what I said, or what he had said, they were afraid of him. He did not go to prison because of anything violent, still they had made this judgment, based on their own fear that they should stay away from him. He was such a sensitive person, that this had a very deep and detrimental impact on him. I talked and talked to the other employees and finally he got invited to a single lunch.

But, as in the earlier interview, he was so paralyzed by the fear he would say the wrong thing he just went along and said nothing at all. So, he was perceived as being standoffish and they did not invite him again. Eventually he quit this job and left the area. I found out months later he had committed suicide. The note he left said he simply had become too afraid of people and too tired of always being afraid to keep living.

It took me years to come to terms with what I felt was the part I played in his death. I thought that if only I had done more to get the other employees to accept him, if only I would have been able to spend more time with him myself (this company had strict rules about people in supervisory roles not socializing with employees).

This is a very drastic and upsetting story about what can happen when someone lives with way too much fear for way too long. This was also a very eye-opening experience for me and I learned a lot about fear and judging people without the benefit of getting to know who they are. I also learned that sometimes people experience fear so deep and all-encompassing they should seek professional help.

Whatever method or methods you decide to employ in working on your fears, you will need to be vigilant in your efforts. This is not an easy process. Keep trying to disprove your fears, and don't lose patience with yourself if you have fearful days. The worst thing you can do is simply try and ignore your fears, you must allow them to be felt, but, you then need to allow them to go away at least to the point where you can do whatever you were afraid of anyway. Sometimes it takes a much longer time to figure out why we fear certain things than we would like it to.

The truth is there is no "quick fix" for learning to handle fear. But, put in the time to do this for yourself and you will find you are stronger and more courageous than you ever believed you were. It took years for these fears to become fully ingrained in your mind; it may well take some time for you to evict them.

If you find along this process you are so very overwhelmed by your fears that they turn into true anxiety or panic attacks, please find someone you can talk to about them. Panic attacks are very real and are not a sign of weakness. Do not let yourself suffer needlessly from your fear-based anxiety or panic attacks; there are many organizations available these days to assist people in handling these issues and many areas have free counseling available as well.

This is truly a more severe thing than simply handling an irrational fear and don't let anyone ever make you feel bad, weak or unworthy because you are fighting this battle. So much of the time, people who do suffer with these issues end up feeling bad for feeling bad, a situation that is very counter-productive and does nothing except perpetrate a never-ending spiral of ill feelings.

Don't be afraid of what anyone else thinks about you or your mental illness; they are only ignorant about your condition and are probably a little afraid of it at the same time. I suffered with panic attacks and severe anxiety for years before I was finally able to slay my own dragons. You can do this as well.

I found very simple things like self-talk, deep breathing and learning to turn my fear-based negative thoughts around to diffuse them were extremely beneficial. It proved helpful to me if I wrote down those things I was afraid of and spent some time evaluating why I was afraid. Once you know what you're really afraid of, it's a lot easier to handle that fear.

Spend some time with you own "fear list" and simply listen to your inner voice explain why you have these fears. Are you afraid of heights, or is it really that you're afraid of falling? If you could be absolutely certain you weren't going to fall, do you think you could maybe take one short glance from the skyscraper viewing deck? Is it that you're afraid of the actual dog, or the bite from a dog? Do you think you could pet a dog that you were absolutely certain would not bite?

Continue this with each of the fears you've written down, follow the "trail" and see where each of your fears really leads you. With the dog bite example above, I would continue that "fear trail" with the following. Why are you afraid of getting bit by a dog? Is it the pain of the bite? Is it that you feel you might have a scar? Are you afraid you might get rabies? Take this as far as you need to, examining each fear until you can't possibly come up with anything further to examine.

Then go back and look at those things you came up with. Reexamine these items. Of all the dogs in the areas I spend time in, about how many of those are likely to bite? What is the chance that in the areas I spend time in, I will encounter one of these dogs that bite? How severe is the typical bite from a dog? About what percentage of all dog bites are in this range of severity? Again, take this as far as you need to go with it. Most likely you will find that even those fears you thought were completely rational have some degree of irrationality in them.

The idea here is to examine your fears to the point where you realize they are only serving to keep you from fully participating in life and not serving you at all to keep you safer.

During the time I was most afraid of life in general I spent a lot of time finding quiet spots in nature where I could simply be alone with my thoughts and feelings; I cried to a lot of rocks and trees during this time about how I felt like a failure because I couldn't seem to control my anxiety. These days, I do this simply to enjoy the calm and nurturing peace of nature. If you're not already in the habit of spending time in nature, you should start.

Let me tell you, rocks and trees are wonderful listeners and I never walked away not feeling a whole lot better. Let's just say I did a lot of emptying my emotional trash at the base of a whole bunch of trees!

A lot of people seem to try and conquer their fears by doing things they are afraid of, and if that's what you want to do, I applaud you for deciding to do so. Please understand though, this is not for everyone and if you know someone you are going to be with has a certain fear, don't try to push them into doing something they do not want to do.

Roller-coasters are a huge fear for many people and I can't tell you how many times I've seen people trying to force others to confront their fears and get on the coaster. This can really have a horrible outcome, even if it's only the fact the friendship will certainly suffer. Everyone has their own stress levels and you could very well push someone well past their limit with dire consequences. Let them tackle their own fears; you have enough of your own to deal with.

Remember that you always have control over your thoughts and actions. You can choose to think positive thoughts or negative ones. Choose to think positively and you will go a long way to overcoming your fears.

Of course, some fears are deeper than others and may take more time to overcome, but stick with it and you'll find you are building more confidence and are better prepared to handle whatever comes your way. This frees you up to live the life you really want, and deserve, to live.

Letting go of the past

I remember distinctly the feeling that I really wanted to just die and get it over with. It was not the first time I had been hit, punched, thrown down or choked until I passed out by my very abusive "at-the-time" husband; but I wanted to make sure it was the last.

Being completely unsupervised and otherwise unguided teenagers, we had managed to become parents before either of us hit the "ripe old age" of 20. So, while the stress and sense of being extremely overwhelmed are very understandable, the constant violence was inexcusable.

I had tried to leave several times, but having no support group, no self-esteem and no place to go, I'd felt I had no choice but to return and try again to make it work. This day, though, felt different. I could no longer bear this constant abuse and remember pleading with whatever higher power existed to please just let him kill me this time.

As I pleaded for my demise, I suddenly became aware of a bright mist in the room and a soothing voice in my head said, "No, you will not die today, today, you will become strong."

Immediately after hearing this voice I knew my life would finally change for the better. Within weeks I had acquired an apartment, via a friend in sudden need of a roommate, a better job and had filed for a divorce.

This would be only my first step along my journey, there would be many, many more trials, much more pain and a lot more self-discovery; but no one would ever physically harm me again and a brand new sense of self and the beginning of my self-esteem and probably more importantly for me, my self-respect, was born.

For years after this experience, and actually after any negative experience anyone around me has ever had, people would say "just let it go" and although I thought I was trying, I finally realized that I didn't really know how to let things go.

After asking a number of others, it became clear that they really didn't know either. There is a big difference between just refusing to think about some negative event that has happened in your life and actually dealing with it so you can really and truly let it go.

It has been the experience of many who have turned to counselors or psychologists, most of whom want to talk about these negative experiences over and over again, that this really doesn't help most people let go of past pain either. So, letting go of something seems to be a very confusing process for a lot of people.

There is a good deal of evidence to support the idea that if you bury negative events and refuse to adequately handle them, eventually, they can manifest in your body and/or mind as disease. Take a look at the word "disease" and you will see this word is comprised of "dis" and "ease."

I know first-hand when I was sick and was in a very negative state of mind I could not seem to get any better regardless of what medications or treatments or surgeries I had.

Yet, once I started meditating and striving to hold onto positive thoughts about my health I started getting much better. I found the same in other people who had gone through similar experiences as my own. Could this be an indication that many of our illnesses are actually caused by our subconscious mind not being at "ease" because of something we've repressed? I cannot prove it for certain, but it is an interesting concept that will be explored a bit deeper in another chapter of this book.

So, exactly how does one let something go? Of course, each one of us is different and what works for me might not work well for you and vice versa. However, the basic premise is pretty much the same for everyone.

First off, really take a look at whatever event has truly derailed, or otherwise upset you. Feel it, see it for what it was, see any part you played and forgive yourself for playing that part.

See what part others played and forgive them also. Really forgive them, don't just "pretend" you've forgiven them. This doesn't mean you have to forgive whatever they did, just forgive the person and not their actions.

Send them love and light wherever they may be. This is important, even if you do not know where they are or haven't seen them for many years. This is important because it signals to the universe or whatever higher power you believe in that you want to receive love and light into your life.

We get back what we send out. Just mentally send love and light to those people who have hurt you. You need to notice that somewhere within this negative event there is a lesson for you to learn.

Be willing to learn that lesson. Tell yourself, the universe, or whatever higher power you personally believe in that you have accepted and learned this lesson and do not need to ever repeat it. Ask your higher power and your subconscious mind to now let this lesson; this event and whoever involved go.

It has helped me to visualize the energy from the negative event flowing from my heart into a balloon, filling the balloon until I feel the negative energy is gone from my being.

I then mentally release the balloon into the universe where universal love and light dissolves the negative energy and sends pure love and light into my heart to take its place.

Once this is done, I give myself hearty congratulations for doing a great job in letting this thing go, and express my gratitude to the universe for taking it away.

There have been times in my life when this visualization just didn't seem to feel quite right to me and I truly felt I needed a more "concrete" method to assist me in letting go of a particularly stubborn negative memory.

In those instances, I wrote down my memory in as much painful detail as I could. I then reread what I had written, drew a big "X" across it and wrote "I am finished with this lesson" across the "X".

Then I went outside to my charcoal grill (now I would use my fire pit, but then that's what I had) and burned the paper. While the paper was burning I visualized the negativity I had been holding on to that was connected with this particular memory burning away inside my subconscious and being replaced with pure love and light.

Of course, my methods are certainly not the only ones that work. I know people who bury eggs at the outside corners of their house to clear negativity, I know people who use incantations, blessings, holy water, sage sticks and any number of other items and/or techniques to help them clear away negativity coming from both inside themselves and outside themselves.

Many people find it helpful to call on their spirit guides, angels, higher power or whatever or whomever you believe in to help them clear away negative thoughts, emotions or memories.

You should feel free to use any or all of these methods as you work to find inner peace and handle those painful memories that keep you from moving forward in your life.

There truly is no one right way to do this, we are all individuals and we are all on our own special path. Find what calls to you and do that. The most important thing is that you do something to take out your trash.

Depending on how severely you were hurt in your negative event, it might take a couple of tries to really and truly feel like you've been successful. You must keep trying until you've managed to free yourself of every negative event you need to let go of.

Harboring negativity only harms you; those that have hurt you do not usually share in your pain. Do yourself a huge favor and let it go, take out your trash. Then you'll be able to fill the spaces in your thoughts previously occupied by negativity with loving, positive thoughts.

Remind yourself that you are not forgiving the actions of whomever caused you pain, you are forgiving the soul of the person. By forgiving them, you allow both of your hearts to release the pain of the past and move forward in love and light.

It is especially difficult to let go of emotional suffering you endured either directly or indirectly at the hands of a parent. In my opinion we have a tendency to overlook this pain simply because a parent was involved. Please free yourself from any and all emotional turmoil your childhood and/or your parents have left in your subconscious.

Do not become disappointed or even surprised when you find yourself letting go of something you really thought you had already let go. Just keep trying, eventually, you will be successful.

There's a funny thing that happens, almost universally, when you start living your life more in line with your true purpose, and I've alluded to it earlier. You will find many people you had thought were close friends, and quite possibly even family members, suddenly start fading away and becoming part of your past instead of your future.

While this can be unsettling, it is not surprising, and you have to remember that this, too, is ok and just part of life. Just because you love someone completely and miss them terribly does not mean they are meant to be a part of your daily life. And, just because someone may have walked alongside you on a path for a very long time, doesn't mean they will always be either on or by your side.

Usually, by the time people reach this point on their journey, they are well aware of who will still be in their daily lives and who will not be around as often as before. Even if you do not consciously think you are aware of this, if you spend some time meditating on it, you will find your subconscious mind certainly is.

This doesn't mean someone is right or someone is wrong, it simply means your paths have gone on in different ways. Many times, someone will come in and out of your life repeatedly over several years, even your entire lifetime.

Other times, someone is simply there for only a short time and then is gone for good. There is a saying that says if something no longer grows corn for you, you need to let it go. I have found that statement also applies to the people in your life, if you have people in your life who consistently bring you down, criticize you or otherwise bring you pain, it is time for you to let them go.

Usually I recommend letting these people simply fade away into your past, but sometimes they will demand to know why you've changed, why you don't hang out like you used to or why you don't call them as much.

When someone habitually points out what "you" did or did not do and neglects to accept any part of whatever is going on it's a pretty clear indication this person is not on a spiritual path and is probably quite selfish. This does not make them a "bad" person it only means they are on a different path than the one you are on.

Refrain from judging them, don't try and get them to see your point or understand your new frame of reference. Just let them know you are seemingly on a different path from their own and some of the things you used to do together no longer fit with what you're interested in doing anymore.

Unfortunately, this can be an unpleasant conversation to have. Sometimes people take these things very personally, and you might have to reassure them this is not a personal attack on them, it is simply that you have developed different interests you want to pursue.

Hopefully they will understand and things will not get any more unpleasant, but unfortunately some people tend towards anger and hostility, especially when they feel they've been personally attacked. While you can reassure them as much as possible this isn't person, many times they will simply choose to believe that it is.

Sometimes they will begin their own spiritual path just out of curiosity, it is probably best not to indulge their questions unless you are certain they are genuinely interested in bettering themselves and not simply in having this in common with you.

Remember to always come from a place of love and light and not from a place of ego and judgment. Whatever you do, please do not let them make you second-guess your own path. Often your own family members will become the most critical, especially if your new path conflicts in any way with the way you were raised.

I've known many people who have felt forced to stop studying spirituality completely because of family members. Please don't allow anyone to make you take any path other than the one your heart and soul tells you to.

Each person comes into our lives for a reason, whether it's to teach us a lesson, show us something about ourselves we were previously unaware of, or simply to love us.

One of the most confusing words in the English language is the word "love". True love is not jealous, it is not possessive, and it is not contingent upon anything. It is most certainly not abusive.

True love is given unconditionally and without any thought to whether or not the "loved" returns the feeling. We love someone because we want to love them, and while it is always nice when they love us in return, we would love them anyway. If you are in a relationship in which love has contingencies or in which you feel forced to be less than your true self, you are not in a loving relationship.

There is a saying that states "be yourself, those who love you will love you anyway and those who don't, never really did." Those are very true words.

Rebuilding, or building for the first time, self-esteem

It is an unfortunate fact that many people have no idea how to be parents, become parents' way before they are ready or have had parents who fit into one or both of these categories. In the case of my parents, and honestly myself as well, it was probably a combination of both of these situations, combined with many other issues.

Keep in mind that no matter how good or bad your childhood was, you do ultimately grow up and become the "boss of yourself." So, whatever excuse(s) you've been giving yourself as a result of having a less than perfect childhood is something you need to get rid of right now.

Nothing you can do right now, at this moment, can change anything about your childhood. You are ultimately in control of your life and have to make the decision to truly take control of your own life from this moment on.

I had a friend who told me, as an adult, that it is never too late to give yourself a happy childhood. This friend was absolutely correct. While you cannot go back, you can rewrite the memories you hold on to and search out the ones than make you feel good instead of all those that make you feel bad.

Each and every one of us, no matter how difficult our childhood was, can find some good memories somewhere in our memory bank. Those are the memories you want to shed light on and hold on to.

I suggest finding one of these memories that really stand out for you. Finding those really funny or good memories from your childhood will go a long way toward helping you feel better about yourself. In my case, I remember the Thanksgiving turkey juggle, it makes me laugh out loud each and every time I think of it.

On this particular Thanksgiving, as usual, my grandmother and mother were busy trying to get food ready at the same time we kids, and other relatives, were busy trying to get a sample of said food. My mother's house was always the location for the "official" family Thanksgiving dinner because we had more room than either my grandmother's or my aunt's house, however, the kitchen itself was very small. In fact, it was probably, way too small for the very large task at hand.

When the turkey was being taken out of the oven, and I don't remember now if it was my mother or my grandmother who initiated this, somehow the turkey slipped out of the pan. Either my mother or grandmother, whichever one was not still holding the now-empty pan, grabbed for the actual turkey.

Being hot, well because it had just been inside an oven, she was unable to fully hold onto the bird; which then bounced into my father's hands as he just happened to walk by. He simply tossed it back into the roasting pan from which it had come.

All of this took place in less than a minute and yet those of who witnessed this event still maintain that it took place in slow motion. Thus the turkey-juggle Thanksgiving story was born.

Through the years, anytime I have caught myself lamenting my less-than-perfect childhood I have relied on this hysterical memory to remind myself that it wasn't all bad.

Most likely, if you've either concentrated on the bad parts of your childhood, or simply have blocked out entire chunks of your childhood, you have a self-esteem problem. You might even say, as I did, that you don't even have any self-esteem at all.

In my case, I never felt like I was good enough, never felt like I fit in and pretty much was ignored, or made fun of, for most of my childhood. While I understood my parents were pretty much overwhelmed with my siblings and just making a living, it still hurt and turned me into a very insecure and self-loathing teenager. I retreated within myself.

I didn't even have enough self-esteem to let anyone know how badly I felt, I just felt lucky they allowed me to live inside and be provided food and clothing. I know that sounds almost funny, but unfortunately, it felt very true to me at that time.

It was not until I had my daughter and had been through my very abusive first marriage and divorce that cost me everything, including my daughter for a time, that I realized the heart of my struggles could be traced back to a lack of self-esteem. As they say, knowing is half the battle, and I started reading, studying and trying to get myself put back together.

At that time there were very few options available to assist battered women and my family was completely non-supportive, so I relied on the couple of friends I'd managed to make and slowly began forming a new way of viewing myself that was positive and loving instead of negative and loathing.

Truthfully, this was a very long and tedious process a portion of which I continue to this day. It seems we, as human beings, are never really "complete."

During this time I realized that I was "missing" large chunks of my childhood. Entire years of my life were just completely gone from my memory. I simply could not remember anything at all, good or bad, about those missing years.

A friend of mine suggested I try hypnosis to see if it would help me recover all of this missing time. This friend was convinced that until I could remember and deal with whatever I was obviously blocking from my conscious memories I would struggle with the same self-esteem issues. I have always considered myself to be extremely lucky that I had this friend around during this time period.

It took several, very in-depth, hypnosis sessions, but eventually I was able to recover most of my missing time. As expected, some of the stuff I had blocked was very upsetting, but mostly it was just seemingly mundane stuff expected from a childhood spent feeling unloved and inadequate.

You might wonder how I would think feeling unloved and inadequate was "mundane" but this truly was how I felt during this time. Honestly, I actually felt lucky I wasn't being beaten or otherwise abused in a home filled with an awful lot of fighting and violence.

On one particular holiday after I had moved away from home I decided to surprise my family with a visit. I walked into the house only to find myself in the midst of one of my brothers chasing another brother with a large knife. Yep, that was a relatively common occurrence.

So, recovering memories from my childhood that were simply about feeling like I was unwanted, unloved and inadequate and not remembering any new ones about being physically harmed was actually freeing.

This was also a huge step for me in building a healthy sense of self-worth and self-love. We are not those things we've experienced, but those things we've experienced have made us who we are. Remember that we all are only capable of doing and acting in a manner in which we feel capable of doing and acting in...in my case, this means I don't "blame" anyone for my childhood.

In each of their own ways, my family was made up of people trying to do the best they felt they could do at the time. And, as I have mentioned earlier, not everything was bad, we had some amazingly funny and often unabashedly silly times interspersed in there as well.

Actually there seemed to be very few times when things were completely calm. Things were either incredibly violent with loud arguing and sometimes physical fighting or the house resembled a comedy club with comedians competing over who could be the funniest and the silliest.

Just like everything else on your journey to being the best "you" you can be building self-esteem requires starting from scratch, letting go of the stuff your subconscious is telling you to be true and replacing the trash with loving, positive thoughts and feelings.

For literally years I lived with positive affirmations taped to every mirror in my house, on the steering wheel in my car and, for a long time, even in my refrigerator. Like any type of exercise, there are good days and bad days and you have to be patient and start slowly or you'll burn out. And, make no mistake, this is exercise. This is a very important exercise in building self love, self confidence and self-esteem.

So, how do you start building or rebuilding your self-esteem? Much research has been done into positive affirmations and I did find them to be of great use in the beginning, if only to help me figure out what to say to myself in order to begin viewing myself in a positive light.

In my case, it helped me to actually write them down myself rather than simply posting a sign or card that was already written, but you certainly wouldn't have to go that far. If you do decide to write the affirmations yourself, I recommend buying some nice paper and colorful pens or markers for this task and making your affirmations the most visually beautiful that you can make them.

As I said before, I put these notes to myself everywhere to make sure I had to see them several times a day. When I first started doing this, I thought it was a rather silly thing to do.

Many of my friends at the time told me how silly they thought it was repeatedly. You might be thinking that now. Take the time and do this for yourself. It really does work, it will not work overnight and you will have to be patient with yourself, but it really will work for you.

The most important affirmation I found for myself was "I am filled with love and light." The reason for this is simply because initially I felt neither love nor light at all, much less being filled with them.

This was the first affirmation I tried and to be honest, it's the only one I still use on a regular basis. I wrote both "you are a wonderful, intelligent person" and "I am a wonderful, intelligent person" on many cards just to make sure my subconscious mind got the message.

I progressed to "I love to eat healthy" once I felt good enough about myself to actually care if I were healthy or not and "I am confident and positive" once I decided I really wanted to rejoin life in general. Another one of my favorites was 'today is a great day.'

When you're just starting to claw your way up out of whatever dark cavern you were in emotionally, having a great day is a huge accomplishment! As I've said before, you might find this silly, and I certainly did too as first; but it did work, I genuinely started feeling better about myself as a result of doing this and I know it will work for you too if you give it a chance.

In talking with friends and clients through the years, as well as via my own experience, I've come to the conclusion that just about everyone experiencing self-esteem issues needs to take more showers and/or long baths. Seriously.

Not simply to be clean in a physical sense, but to feel better. Literally washing off the negative energy, vibes, thoughts, whatever label you would like to use. For whatever reason, when people have a very low opinion of themselves, they tend not to take care of themselves. In my opinion this is because they do not feel as though they are worthy of being taken care of. So, I found it to be very therapeutic to take a long shower, or long hot bath at the end of each day, and especially on those days when I really didn't feel like it.

Each time I would visualize all the negativity leaving me, all the self-loathing thoughts, everything bad that had ever happened to me, all being washed down the drain. Again, I know it sounds like a silly thing to do, but it worked for me and it's worked for many friends and clients I've spoken with through the years. And, it's a very simple thing to do.

Probably a more popular and effective choice than to take a long, hot shower is to take a long, hot, fragrant bath. While you can certainly choose whatever scents you like and are drawn to, certain fragrances like lavender and vanilla are known for their calming and soothing qualities.

Bath salts are readily available and you can probably find one you really like. I prefer to make my own with pure essential oils and either sea salt or Epsom salts. This allows me to customize my exact fragrance and I can make as much or as little as I want each time.

If you have very dry or sensitive skin, you might want to forgo the salts completely and just experiment with a few drops of a pure essential oil in your bathwater; just make sure to use only the pure essential oil as some synthetic fragrance oils can be irritating to sensitive skin.

Personally, my favorite scent is a mixture of lavender and mint, but experiment and I'm sure you will find your own favorites. Whatever scent you choose, you can add to your experience with candles, incense and/or soft music.

I always advise people to breathe deeply, relax and visualize the negativity leaving their body, heart and mind. Whenever you are ready to get out of your bath visualize this negativity going down the drain.

Of course, you can also mix a bit of essential oil with some very warm water in a spray bottle and use that in the shower as well. This also makes a very nice room spray and I've used this for years as an aromatherapy technique for both myself and for others. All of these are very simple and inexpensive things that will help you feel better and hold on to positive thoughts. Think of it as you pampering you like you deserve to be pampered!

When you've been able to do something you've never thought you'd be able to do, or you realize one day that you're really starting to like yourself, it's a cause for a celebration. I used to write myself congratulatory cards when I'd had a good day. I went to a dollar store and bought a package of very inexpensive colored paper and some markers and each time I had something to celebrate I would make myself a card.

Initially, this was a very difficult thing for me to do and it took me quite a while to make the first ones, but eventually, it actually became a very fun thing and it is one thing I now have life coaching clients do for themselves.

You will find that these little things you do for yourself add up over time to a much healthier self-esteem! Sort of like a more formal and personalized written affirmation with a twist of congratulations thrown in for good measure. Sometimes it is the seemingly silliest things that can have the greatest impact...at least on me.

At one time I had a boss who had just a really abrasive personality; he walked all over everyone in the office. I had really been working on myself for quite a while and one day he said something very derogatory to me. This was not unusual, as he did this every day, not only to me, but to everyone who worked there.

This particular day though I had the courage to stand up for myself and I told him that what he said was very rude and I would appreciate it if he did not say anything like that to me again. Not only did he not have anything to say in response, but he didn't say anything derogatory to me again for the duration of his employment there.

This not only made me feel better about myself, it showed my co-workers they could also stand up to this boss. We actually went out to lunch together in celebration of this event. Over the next several months, he became less and less abrasive and although he was far from a "nice guy" he certainly became a lot more tolerable.

Eventually he left the company and not too long after he left actual legislation was put into effect prohibiting some of the things this particular boss had been doing and saying for years. I've often thought about the timing of these laws with his leaving.

One area of personal growth that I really don't feel gets enough attention is that you need to learn to be honest with yourself. You have to be cognizant of your motivations for undertaking this journey you are now on. Whatever those motivations are, they are the perfect motivations for you at this time in your life.

I know many people who have undertaken self-improvement journeys and even spiritual journeys because they wanted to be rich. At least they were being honest. The funny thing is that somewhere along their journeys seeking wealth, they realized they already were wealthy, just maybe not in a monetary sense.

Further, they came to realize that money wasn't really what they wanted at all; they really wanted what they thought having that money would do for them. Eventually, one of these people became an energy healer who often works on a voluntary basis and the other is now a teacher.

Does either of these people think they failed along their journey because they didn't become fabulously wealthy? Nope, to the contrary, they both feel extremely successful and, yes, even wealthy, only a deeper more satisfying type of wealth that either one of them will tell you is worth more than any amount of money or riches.

I tell you that story just so you will realize that whatever has motivated you to become the best version of "you" that you can be is the right one for you. The universe knew exactly what to say to get your attention and put you on this path.

Will your visions of your future change as you move forward? Undoubtedly as you grow and change, you will become more attuned to what your true purpose, your true calling on this planet is and you will move toward that direction.

For right now, thank whatever thought, feeling, emotion, circumstance or situation that brought you to this point and give yourself a hug for being brave enough to take the first few steps.

Always take the time to treat yourself. You are a wonderful, loving, inspiring person who deserves to have a favorite treat from time to time. The treat does not have to relate to food, and it's actually much better if it isn't edible.

In my case, I would treat myself to a scented candle, incense or fresh flowers from time to time. Make sure you choose something that has a special meaning for you. This doesn't have to be a big or expensive item, just something small; a present from you to you. This can even be a free something, like a walk on the beach or a trip to a favorite park.

You could even take yourself out to a movie. Spend a bit of time thinking about it and I bet you can come up with all sorts of ways to treat yourself special! I can't emphasize enough how very important this is for you to do, it will have a huge impact on how you see yourself and on how others see you as well. No one is ever going to really care more about you than you care about yourself.

One very large step on the road to a healthy self-esteem is to take care of yourself. This means you need to eat healthy, get enough sleep, exercise, take vitamins, and meditate; whatever you need in order to be the healthiest person you can be is what you need to do for yourself.

Studies have shown that exercise, and actually even simply being outside, makes people feel better. Make going for a walk outside or riding a bicycle a regular part of your life. Try to find a secluded place outside where you can meditate undisturbed.

Commit to doing these things as often as you can for a minimum of 30 days and you will be amazed at how much better you feel about yourself. Keeping small commitments like these will go a long way to building your self-esteem.

In the beginning of my journey, I was horribly strapped for cash and really felt I couldn't afford to eat healthy. What I found was that if I only shopped the outer aisles in the grocery store, and ate a mostly plant-based diet, I actually ended up spending less that I had been and I was certainly eating healthier! I have also found shopping at farmer's markets in my area is a great way to get terrific produce at amazing prices. Shop around to find the best deals in your area, but don't think that just because you don't have a lot of cash you can't eat healthy.

Of course, I've also raised chickens for some time and I've found that I'm able to barter extra eggs for produce at the farmer's market. Don't underestimate the power of a simple backyard or patio garden either, one tomato plant yields an amazing amount of tomatoes and salad greens and zucchini are prolific as well.

In many areas there are even community gardens where you can grow your own veggies and this also offers a chance to meet new friends and perhaps barter what you're growing for what they're growing. Plus you're getting in some exercise as well! It's a win-win.

Personally, I found eating a healthier diet had the biggest impact on my overall outlook on life. By getting my weight under control a multitude of other health issues also got under control and many of these eventually went away altogether.

Once you get to the point where you are getting outside for a while every day, doing some light exercise like walking or biking and eating a healthy diet, you'll find you are also sleeping better at night, better able to meditate, and generally a happier, more confident person.

Each of these areas builds on the next and they are all important. Most likely, you won't even remember all those negative things you used to think about yourself. Or, if you do remember them, you realize those thoughts were simply not true. You will get to a point where you look back at your life and will hardly recognize yourself as you used to be. This will sneak up on you, and you won't realize it's happening while you're going through the process, but it will happen.

You are one of a kind, you would not be here on this earth at all if there was another "you," so treat yourself well, believe in yourself and love yourself. Start right now by taking some deep breaths and mentally congratulating yourself for getting to the point you are at right this very minute.

There are still days I catch myself thinking that I can't do something, or I wouldn't be good at something. Everyone encounters their nerves from time to time. But, I've learned that I really can do anything I put my mind to and while I may not do it perfectly, I will certainly give it my very best effort. The overwhelming majority of the time, my best effort is way more than enough. You will find the same is true about yourself.

Are we really making ourselves sick?

Certainly there are few manners of thinking more controversial than the one that says illness is created by those who are suffering from the illness. Detractors from this line of thought say it simply is a 'blame the victim' mentality and isn't fair to people who are dealing with critical and often, life-threatening diseases.

Yet, throughout history, many cultures including those of traditional China and Tibet, have taught that diseases have an emotional connection and therefore, an emotional cure within each of us. And, if we are honest, we have all experienced an upset stomach or maybe sweaty palms and/or a rash when we've been extremely nervous or upset; or maybe a headache when we're worried about the outcome of a project or the impending serious discussion with a parent, child, friend or spouse.

Doesn't this clearly show our thoughts and feelings DO have an impact on our health, even if usually it is only on a temporary basis? Since our thoughts and beliefs are the source of our emotions, it therefore stands to reason that if what we think and believe to be true can make us sick, what we think and believe can also make us healthy.

In recent years, even many western physicians are coming around to the belief that the thoughts and emotional states of their most critically-ill patients can have an impact on the outcome of the patients' treatments and ultimately their disease.

How often have you, personally, heard the story of someone who had been given a diagnosis that included a little-to-no possibility of survival? These cases abound.

So, how is it that these people undergo almost miraculous cures when others, often with much less serious diagnoses, succumb to their diseases? What makes these people different? What gives them an edge over someone else? The people I know who fall into this category have all said they credit their positive mental outlook, the practice of meditation and visualizing themselves being in perfect health and the love, support and positive outlooks of those closest to them. While this is hardly indisputable scientific evidence, you have to admit it does look as though there is something to this way of thinking.

Of course, the opposite is also true. Through the course of my volunteer work with people who were either abused as children or suffered from spousal abuse I found many very young people suffering from ulcers, chronic headaches and other, some very serious, issues.

You might wonder, as I did at first, exactly how does an otherwise healthy 12-year-old end up with an ulcer? Or, how does a seemingly healthy and vibrant 22-year-old end up with daily headaches and a rash that proved almost untreatable even with prescription medication, dietary changes and the ruling out of any skin allergies?

These are only two instances when western medicine failed to find a reason for the afflictions suffered by people who had endured some type of trauma. Of course, this doesn't mean these people, these victims, consciously caused their ailments, but you have to consider the affect the constant stress of their living conditions had on their emotions, thoughts and beliefs and therefore on their health.

In one particular case, one previously-battered wife's ailments completely went away without medical intervention once she removed herself from the abusive situation and started working with an energy practitioner and subsequently meditating on healing her painful past.

Of course, and she herself would be the first to tell you, if you have serious medical issues you should consult a physician and not simply rely on positive thoughts to heal you. I really think that finding a balance between modern medicine and ancient healing works the best.

Personally, I suffered greatly during my own experience with abuse. By the time I was 24 I, too, suffered from a bleeding stomach ulcer, headaches and a borderline eating disorder, the particulars of which I will spare you.

The stress my daily trauma had taken on me and my health was so great it took a great many years for me to completely heal my emotional state through energy work, visualization and meditation; with the assistance of a great many wonderful practitioners, healers and teachers.

So, I know this works, it worked for me, and whether or not you've personally walked this path for any portion of your life, I know it will work for you too.

No matter what your health situation is at this very moment, mentally thank your body for simply working as well as it is right now. When I was trying so desperately to get healthy, this was a huge part of my daily regimen.

I had a mental checklist I went through every morning, even before I got out of bed. First, I would pay attention to any pain I felt. I would say "I'm sending love and healing light to (whatever part of my body was hurting)." At this point I was not yet very good at visualizing, so I just said the words.

After I had taken my private pain inventory I would take some deep breaths and say "today is a great day" and "every day in every way I am getting healthier and healthier." This was my first-thing-every-day task for many, many months.

As I actually started feeling less and less pain and had more and more great days I would routinely change my morning affirmations as I felt like it. I do still say 'today is a great day' almost every morning to this day...it just makes me feel good.

Feeling good mentally is a very large part of staying well physically. I found that when I didn't feel good mentally I didn't eat very well even when good food was in the house. I also found that when it was more difficult for me to find the time to exercise, I felt a lot more pain and it was really hard for me to do things like meditate or even just go outside for some fresh air. We really do need to take care of our body, mind and soul and keep them in balance all the time. Knowing is half the battle, still it is only "half" the battle.

Once I really "got" how much better I felt when I made myself go out and do these things I found the motivation to do so. Of course, everyone gets sick at one time or another and I am certainly not suggesting that everyone gets sick because they have negative thoughts or emotions they haven't dealt with.

I just know that having a positive attitude, no matter what you have to do to give yourself one, does have an amazing impact on your health. It's sort of a self-fulfilling prophecy...you need to feel good so you take care of yourself so you will feel good. Now, that is a pretty good merry-go-round to get on!

So, are we really making ourselves sick? Personally, I think this is a debate that will continue for quite a while. I completely get why people do not want to think those they care about, particularly victims of abuse and/or neglect, might be negatively impacting their own health and I understand fully why people are unable or unwilling to take responsibility for the idea that what they think has a direct impact on their own health.

Still, if you could make yourself well, or healthier, simply by thinking more positively, why wouldn't you at least try to do it?

Do I really have to learn to meditate to have a great life?

Throughout this book so far I've mentioned a variety of ways you can find peace and love within yourself. None of these ways, in my opinion, is more important than meditating.

I'm sure you've heard about the benefits of meditation for many years and simply tossed those ideas aside as some sort of "new age mumbo jumbo." I'm sure of this because there was a time I did the same thing. What I came to learn is not only is it easy to meditate once you get the hang of it, the results you get from the practice in the form of more peace of mind, more clarity, better ability to focus, better ability to sleep deeply at night and awaken more refreshed in the morning and so many more health benefits; make meditation so vitally important I believe it should be taught in elementary schools. Seriously.

Many people are under the mistaken belief that meditation takes a long time to learn, takes too long to actually do in the first place and requires a special place, wearing special clothing and sitting in a special position on a special mat, saying special words or syllables.

Yes, you could do all, some or actually none of these things. Truly, none of these things are really necessary from a practical meditation standpoint. Yes, there are enlightened yogis who have been meditating for many hours per day for many decades in order to attain their enlightened state. You, however, are probably not ever going to be an enlightened yogi, so you truly do not need this type of devotion in your meditation practice.

Really all you need is a quiet place where you will not be disturbed and a few minutes of your time. Most people begin meditating for just a few minutes at a time because it does take some time and practice to learn to quiet your mind. If you start out by trying to meditate for 20 minutes or longer, you will only frustrate yourself and give up. Start slowly and you will be able to get tremendous benefits from meditation before you know it.

Ok, you've located your quiet place, now what? Sit quietly in whatever position you find comfortable. You do not have to sit on the floor or ground, you can sit in a chair, on a bench or even in your car. Just find a comfortable position. Take a deep breath.

Breathe in through your nose and out through your mouth, try letting your breath take twice as long to leave your body as it does when you inhale. Visualize the breath coming into your body and filling up your lungs then flowing out of your body, taking all your stress, pent-up energy and/or negative thoughts with it.

For some, it helps to visualize your breath entering your body as a white mist and exiting as a grey or even black mist. This seems to help some people relax and let go of their stress and any negative thoughts or emotions they have at the time. If you can't quite visualize your breath yet, that's ok, just think it.

Take three or four of these deep cleansing breaths then visualize a white light coming down from the heavens, entering through the top of your head and moving all the way down your spine, eventually leaving through the bottoms of your feet, and anchoring you to the earth.

Again, if you are not good with visualizing yet, that is fine, just believe there is a white light coming down from the heavens, entering the top of your head and moving down your body to anchor you to the earth. If you do this correctly you can feel this energy in your body.

It might take several attempts, but eventually you will feel it. Most people feel a warm tingly sensation; others simply feel a deep sense of calm and peace. At this point you should be relaxed and completely calm. Concentrate on your deep breaths and feel the loving universal energy coursing through your body.

If you have thoughts pop into your head, and you will, just notice them and let them fade away. Many people find it helps them to mentally say, 'ok, I'll think about that later' to each thought that pops up. Others simply return their concentration to their deep breathing. Whatever works best for you is what you should do.

Initially try to sit and quiet your mind for just a couple of minutes, twice each day. Most people who meditate regularly do so both morning and evening and some do so more often. Find what schedule works best for you and it is perfectly fine if you can't keep a regular schedule; you don't have to meditate at the same exact time every day if that doesn't work with your other life commitments. Many people try to use this as an excuse for why they can't meditate and it simply is not one.

From my experience in talking to people who meditate on a regular basis the average length of time for actively meditating is about 20 minutes twice a day. Of course, many people meditate for much longer and others find they can only handle about 10 minutes before they need to stop.

Your meditation practices will also vary according to what is going on in your life at the time. People find it helpful to meditate either more often or for longer time periods if they are under extreme stress, or if they have a difficult project at work or home they are in the midst of. Many people also vary their meditations if they're feeling anxious or nervous about the outcome of a particular situation.

As you get more proficient in meditation, you will find you can give yourself 'time-outs' during the day whenever you feel stressed or sad or just need a break from whatever you're doing. At this point you won't even need to go through your entire process, you will be able to find your center and refocus your mind almost immediately.

If you find, after seriously trying to meditate for a while, that you are unable to quiet your mind at all, you may find saying "om" or another sound, helpful in keeping other thoughts from popping up constantly. It really doesn't matter what particular sound you choose, as long as it helps you.

Some people turn their meditation time into affirmation time by coming up with a very simple one or two words that has great meaning to them. I know someone who repeats the word "love" over and over while they meditate; others use "peace" or even "confidence." Choose something that has a particular meaning to you, and feel free to change it up occasionally.

If you still find you are struggling, it might be good for you to try a guided meditation. There are many very good ones available and you can probably even find some for free on the internet that work well for you.

Another method of meditation is active meditation. Many runners or people who go for long walks actually achieve a meditative state while running or walking. While I am not a runner, many friends who are have talked about the "runner's high" which really seems like it could certainly be considered meditation to me.

Others swear by activities like knitting, fishing or even playing solitaire. Pretty much any activity you engage in completely to the exclusion of anything and/or everyone else could be considered meditating.

There is an almost limitless amount of choice available to you and I'm sure you will find something that speaks to you. While I do know people who even meditate on feelings of sadness and anger, I really doubt they're finding inner peace when they do this. I highly encourage you to do your best to try and be as positive as possible during your meditations.

If you do find yourself being constantly barraged with negative thoughts and/or feelings during meditating it might be helpful to stop and try again later when you've had a chance to calm down and/or come to a peace with these thoughts. Or try and find a guided meditation with a focus on positivity and/or letting go or negativity.

Often times, people who are suffering with mild depression, anxiety or panic attacks experience a sense of dread while trying to meditate and almost feel as though they come under attack from negative thoughts. If you identify with this, please understand you are not alone as this is very common.

I personally found the trick to dealing with this situation to be continually reminding myself these thoughts were not true, I did not want them to be true and they never would be true. Initially, I also found it helpful to take a walk or get some other exercise before trying to meditate. Sometimes people find it helpful to burn incense or candles or listen to soft soothing music.

Many people find yoga is extremely beneficial when you are just starting out with meditation. And if you've never tried Tai Chi, I highly recommend it.

The ultimate benefit you will get from meditating so greatly outweighs any of the difficulties you initially have in learning to meditate. Meditation is so very worth your time and effort I feel it's imperative to find something that will help you along your way.

Once you are able to fully experience a deep meditation you will understand what I'm saying and you'll wonder how you ever got through your days without this wonderful tool.

Something that is really not covered in books about meditation, and I've never even known personally of it being taught in a class, is the effect of actual clinical depression and other serious mental illnesses on meditation.

I'm not talking about someone who is going through a period of feeling very sad or who has gone through some sort of emotional trauma and is feeling a depressed mood. This refers to someone who has been or is currently truly clinically depressed, or is suffering from another mental illness and is likely under the care of a physician and may or may not be on prescribed medications for their condition.

If you are currently clinically depressed, suffer from schizophrenia have been diagnosed with another type of mental illness or are bi-polar you should consult with your therapist or physician before trying to begin meditating. While anyone can feel negative thoughts when they first attempt to meditate, this is greatly exaggerated in those with a mental illness and could make things much worse.

I did know someone years ago who actually did attempt suicide as a result of going into a very deep meditative state while on prescription medication for clinical depression. So please, check with your doctor if you feel this might apply to your situation.

Understand that meditation is meant to be a positive and calming experience. If what you feel is anything other than positive, loving and calming, please stop, handle whatever emotional turmoil you are experiencing and try again later. There is no shame in recognizing you aren't ready to proceed with something, you can always come back to it at a later time.

Using Music in Meditation

By now I'm sure everyone has become aware of the healing qualities of music. Whether your personal tastes tend to favor soothing nature music or heavy metal music, it's not a secret that music makes us feel better. Just conduct an internet search for meditation music and you'll find more music than you probably will ever have time to listen to.

And, as I've said before, just about anything you put 100 percent of your mind and energy on can be considered meditation. So, while one person likes to do yoga with soft and soothing music in the background someone else might like to listen to much harder sounding rock music to motivate them through their run. Yet, both of these people are experiencing the benefits of using music and both of these activities could certainly be considered meditative in nature.

Much has been written and talked about in regards to the many varieties of meditation music with subliminal messages currently available. While I'm certainly not an expert in such things, I have used some of them myself with varying degrees of success. I do know many people who absolutely swear by them and who am I to tell these people they're wrong.

Bottom line, if this is something that speaks to you and that you find comforting or otherwise appealing, by all means use these recorded tracks.

I do know that if music is what makes you actually sit down and try to meditate then it is well worth it. Many people begin their meditation practice by listening to soft music and gradually find they come to a point in time where they no longer need to use music at all. They have come to realize they appreciate the total silence more than the music, no matter how soft and soothing it is. Others would never even consider meditating without their music.

The thing I will caution you about though is to pick your music carefully. Unless you are using an activity as your form of meditation, running or jogging for example, you will want a very soft and soothing form of music playing as you try to calm your mind.

This is one time you really don't need something loud, angry or fast; you simply will not get the desired effect, unless of course, you want to meditate about being angry. And, I do know people who really and truly believe you can meditate about anger, frustration, or any other emotion just as easily and effectively as you can meditate about peace, love and well-being.

Their feeling is that by focusing in on their negative emotions they come to a sort of peace with those emotions and then can let them go. While their take on meditation doesn't really match my own as I utilize meditation as a way to calm my mind and focus on positive things; I cannot say their views on meditation are wrong.

Certainly I do not think I would benefit from trying their form of meditation, but if this is something that feels right to you, again, who am I to say it's wrong.

My favorite method of incorporating music into meditation is drumming. It doesn't matter what type of drums you use, there's just something about a steady drum beat that is very calming to me.

It's as if I'm listening to the heart beat of the universe when I'm drumming. Of course, I'm talking about a single drum, or a drum circle, with hand drums and not the large drum set of a rock band; although I do know people who find that particular type of drumming calming as well.

Drum circles are very popular in many places, so if you feel this is something you would like to experience I'm sure you can locate a group relatively close to your location. Really there's nothing quite like a large drum circle in perfect synchronicity to connect you with a higher power, at least in my opinion. I'm certain if you look for them you can find recordings of hand drums that would also accomplish the same thing without you having to take up drumming yourself.

However, you decide to meditate, whether you decide to use music, subliminal messages or even if you decide to meditate on your anger, the important thing is that you make a sincere effort to form a habit of meditating each and every day. This is one habit that is well worth the time to create!

Learn to use visualization

As I've mentioned previously in this book, I have used visualization techniques in order to bring about positive changes in my life. You've no doubt heard about visualization from a variety of sources, ranging from that guy you know and never thought much of to the latest guru on TV telling you this is the way to cure all your ills.

Truthfully, visualization is as wonderful or as awful as you make it. Very simply put, visualization is a technique whereby you manufacture a picture of your ideal life in your mind, putting as much detail and emotion into it as possible, and hold that thought for at least several minutes. A lot of people say you should do this several times a day and others say once a day is sufficient.

Many people like to project their images on an internal movie screen and that's a wonderful technique if that's what works for you. Visualization is really pretty much make-believe for grown-ups. I have used this technique myself and find it to be at minimum a very positive experience and there are some things I know for certain I would never have found the courage to do without first visualizing them.

Unfortunately, many so-called experts have lead many people to believe this is a quick fix for whatever is wrong in your life. This has made many people who would otherwise find something positive in this technique quite literally run for the hills whenever anyone mentions it as a possibility.

I really do think this is something that has enough value in it that you do owe it to yourself to at least give it a try. So, then, what is the most effective way to utilize visualization?

Most often I have found it beneficial to start with something you really would like, but is small enough that you are not completely emotionally attached to the outcome. This is because we're trying to build confidence and courage here, along with your self-esteem, to allow you to make positive changes in your life. Like elsewhere in this book, I'm talking baby steps here. If you start small while you are learning, you have a much better chance of having these small steps be successful. This will give you the confidence you need in order to take bigger steps.

Usually I like to start out with my life coaching clients by having them simply visualize what a great day would look like, be like and feel like. Really see yourself having an awesome day. What is this like for you? What time would you get up in the morning? What would you eat for breakfast, what would you wear, what would you do, where would you go, who would you see, etc.?

Truly give it some thought, create images to back up your thoughts and really let yourself feel what this day would be like for you. By creating something simple such as a great day in your current life, in your current location and with those things, activities and people you are already familiar with you take away the disbelief and the fear that can accompany visualizations for people just beginning to use that technique.

This will also help you to start forming mental images because you will already be familiar with your subject matter. Once you become good at visualizing the place you live right now in your mind's eye, you can move on to creating new images for your future.

Many times, if you listened to guided visualizations, they want you to see yourself in a grand house, in a grand location and with money, cars and all the trappings of a luxurious lifestyle. And, that is wonderful once you feel comfortable seeing yourself in that light.

However, in my experience, I found those images someone else was trying to create for me to be so vastly different and foreign from the life I knew that I just simply didn't believe those images or that life could actually belong to me. Honestly, many of those visualizations other people were trying to create for me weren't even things that I wanted and they certainly weren't things that motivated me to take any action at all.

After listening to several of these recordings, I just decided maybe this visualization stuff wasn't really for me at all. I just didn't believe this imagination stuff was worth my time, I couldn't ever really be "that" person. Of course, this goes back to a self-esteem issue, but isn't that what we're really trying to address here anyway?

So, be kind to yourself and start small. To someone who has been neglected/abused/sick/injured or whatever your personal path has been, simply visualizing a good day is a huge thing.

Once I realized I could just do that, and that I really did not have to visualize "the whole world at my feet" I finally embraced this technique as something worthwhile. You will find that by successfully visualizing one good day after another, things really will start changing for you.

You start to believe this thing really works. When you do find something happens that didn't go quite to your visualized plan, you'll be better able to just say "ok, that wasn't what I wanted" and rewrite your plan on the fly.

Once you find this is all working well for you, by all means, mentally create that awesome life with those awesome cars, people and places! By the time you are ready to do that, you'll really believe you CAN be "that person."

A huge part of visualization is very similar to meditation in that it's a tool for you to use in order to bring yourself back to a peaceful state. If you feel comfortable visualizing yourself on the beach when you are actually sitting at your desk in your office, do that.

Even giving yourself "mini-mental-vacations" of just a couple of minutes at a time can be enough to bring your stress levels down. Just be careful you don't spend so much time daydreaming you don't get any work done at all. Trust me that will certainly NOT lower your stress levels!

I'm often asked "what is really the difference between visualization and simple day-dreaming?" To me, you can engage in day-dreaming almost constantly through your day, almost simultaneously with whatever else you're doing. For example, who hasn't been sitting at work, even in a meeting wondering what they were going to do for lunch or dinner? Or driving to work or school thinking about the weekend and what plans they had or would make? Day-dreaming requires no emotional attachment at all, no mental imagery and actually very little active thinking.

Visualization requires all of these in order to be successful. Engaging your emotions, mental imagery and actively thinking about your visualization is what gives it energy in your subconscious mind. Whatever your mind believes to be true is what you are likely to manifest in your life.

Visualization is an active method of creating the plan you want your life to follow, the things you want your mind to believe to be true; therefore, you need to become fully engaged in that plan.

Of course, if you normally day-dream about things you really want in your life; you can always create a wonderful and very effective visualization around those day-dreams.

I've personally used visualization for everything from eating a healthier diet to putting together benefit events. Sometimes, letting yourself really 'get into' a particular visualization can show you ways to succeed you weren't even consciously thinking about.

For example, when I was thinking about one particular benefit event, I created a very vivid visualization about how the event would unfold, how successful it would be, who would help me, etc. At one point during my active visualization, a thought popped into my head about a particular commercial I had recently seen.

Because of this, I contacted that company, was put in touch with one of the partners in the company and eventually got a very nice donation and a lot of free press and other assistance with the promotion of my event.

Had I not been actively visualizing the success of this event, I doubt the thought to contact this company that was seemingly unrelated to, and therefore, in my mind uninterested in my benefit, would have ever occurred to me at all.

Personally, I have found the "trick" to visualization is to start with something you truly and honestly believe can actually happen. Don't worry or even think about "how" this could happen, just accept the fact it will. After a while, you will find it's easier to accept the fact that "bigger" things can happen in your life as well. You start to "stretch" your mind in new ways of seeing your life, your world and really in how you see yourself.

Once you get comfortable with the thought you really can have or do whatever it is you would really like, or even whoever you want to be, your subconscious mind will go along with you.

Remember not to visualize the "hows" just visualize the outcome. If you truly dedicate yourself to this process, you will find, like I have, ideas just start popping into your head. Those ideas may very well turn into your "hows."

One caution about visualization though...is to be very careful that your visualizations don't simply become a daydream. Visualization is an amazing technique; however, it does require some work from you. You can't just sit around all day doing nothing except thinking about how you wish your life was, that isn't visualization, that's a daydream. While you can certainly make visualizations out of your daydreams, you can't really manifest anything through daydreaming by itself, except for a waste of time.

Visualization puts the universe on notice that this is what you want, so the universe will bring opportunities to you that will bring those things you want into your life. You still have to take advantage of those opportunities. I've heard many people complain about how visualization doesn't work for them when upon further questioning it seems they've never once taken advantage of an opportunity that was placed right in front of them.

Make sure you actually make an effort before simply dismissing something as not working for you. Visualization most certainly works, if you allow it to work, if you believe it works and if you are willing to take advantage of the opportunities you will manifest into your life.

Love and light?

What, exactly, is this "love and light" everyone keeps talking about?

The first time I heard the phrase, which has recently become a popular "blessing" in spiritual circles, "love and light" was in connection with what I was told was a Buddhist teaching that says we should see everyone and everything through a loving and accepting eye.

Basically, to honor everyone's path regardless of what belief system their path consists of. More recently, people have taken to using love and light as a general spiritual greeting, meaning something along the lines of 'may the light of the Source always shine in your heart and may you be filled with universal love.'

You also need to realize that our "paths" consist of more than simply our spiritual and/or religious beliefs. Our paths are made up of absolutely everything in our lives and every single aspect of that 'everything'.

There are so many people who are ready and able to accept various spiritual paths, even those vastly different from their own, yet are somehow unable to accept someone who is gay, lesbian or transgender. Or there are even people who still cannot accept those of a different race than their own.

As a society, we attach all types of labels to people, especially people we perceive to be different from ourselves. To truly live in "love and light" we should see people as simply being people and not as whatever label we might put on them.

Acceptance of every aspect of everyone's path is an absolute necessity and a huge piece of the meaning behind the phrase "love and light." You are probably thinking that you already are completely accepting of everyone and that is truly wonderful if you are.

But, pay attention to how you react to those who are different. Did you have a fleeting thought of maybe you should take a wider path around that guy with all the piercings and tattoos that passed you on the sidewalk? Were you momentarily hesitant to smile back at that homeless person who smiled at you as you walked past? Did you automatically avert your eyes when that woman in the grocery store moved past you to reach something on a shelf simply because she was dressed according to a different culture? Did you catch yourself wondering if you were safe when you were getting gas and a group of motorcycle riders pulled into the gas station?

Even if you're consciously making the sincerest of efforts to be as open and accepting as possible, there's probably a time or two you can remember when you really weren't. That's ok, just notice it, forgive yourself and always try to do better than before. Many of our prejudices are so deeply ingrained within our psyche it takes a very concerted effort simply to notice that we even have them.

Every day, try to engage someone who is vastly different from you in an open and honest conversation for at least a couple of minutes. Really take the time to try to get to know and understand this person's views in this short amount of time. You will find it an eye-opening experience that will truly enrich your life.

Unfortunately it seems as though many are simply saying the words "love and light" without understanding exactly what they mean...it's become the "spiritual trendy" greeting. What a wonderful world we would inhabit if more people really understood this greeting and truly believed and fully embraced what it means!

Of course, everyone has a slightly different take on what these words mean, and I am not saying any one version of the definition is more correct than another. Simply put, in my mind, 'love and light' is a blessing from one spiritual being to another, spoken or written with the hope that the one the blessing is bestowed upon is filled with compassion, acceptance, forgiveness and a loving nature for the universe.

It is meant to be a positive and loving affirmation that we are all on the path to becoming the best version of ourselves we can be, and even though we might not share the same path, or have the same beliefs, we love and accept one another, exactly how we are in our current state. We realize none of us are perfect, but we're all imperfect together.

In view of this, my hope for you is that you learn to truly love and accept yourself, with all your flaws and attributes; and extend that same love and acceptance to everyone else.

If we all spent more time learning to love and accept ourselves, humanity as a whole would be a whole lot more peaceful. Instead of always looking at and pointing out those things that make us different, we should be striving to find common ground and focusing on those things that make us all the same.

There is a poster I've recently seen with a baby on it and the caption says something like "you see a biker, I see grandpa." While I chuckled when I saw it, the truth of the matter is that as people, we still make rash judgments on other people based solely on how we choose to see them at any given moment.

I can't tell you how many truly awesome, caring, loving people I know who are motorcycle riders, or are covered in tattoos and/or piercings, have different religions and/or cultures, or who are trans, gay, lesbian, bi-sexual or simply dress differently than most...the list goes on and on.

My point here is simply that you can't really expect other people to treat you with love and light unless you're willing to do the same.

I've heard way too many people talk about how they're on this great path to enlightenment (whatever that really means) and then they turn right around and say something horribly derogatory about someone else. They use the phrase 'love and light' as if they're ordering a coffee or saying 'the light is green.' Without passing judgment, it really seems as if maybe these people might have some trash to take out.

Personally I think these types of people are the primary reason spirituality as a whole has sort of a bad rap in some areas. It is sort of like the guy, who goes to the bar, gets drunk, goes home and beats his wife on Saturday night but then he goes to church on Sunday so he thinks he's an awesome guy with deep spirituality.

Of course, each of these people is on their own path and we should simply wish them well and leave them be no matter how difficult that can seem to do; but maybe these aren't really the best role models for "love and light". Please, if you're going to talk the talk, walk the walk.

What is spirituality anyway?

I really think spirituality means many different things to many different people; in fact, there are probably just about as many definitions of what spirituality really is as there are people. When I think about spirituality, I think about the interconnectedness of every being in the universe with each other as well as with a higher source.

Whatever name you have for the higher source, is fine for you and fits your path at this time perfectly. Too often I think people get so caught up with "religion" they forget to pay attention to "spirituality." While certainly spirituality should be a part of whatever religion you practice, I don't think spirituality by itself is actually connected to any particular religion at all.

Spirituality is something within each of us, it is that thing that makes us know that without a doubt we are a part of something larger than what we can see and understand.

Spirituality is that special spark inside each of us that says we should help those less fortunate, take care of the sick and elderly, try to heal our planet and try our very best to be as loving, accepting and kind as we can possibly be.

Most likely you have experienced something similar to the following story, and it shows just how very differently different people view religion and spirituality. I just happened to be at a very busy street fair with an enormous number of vendors when I started hearing shouting.

As I continued walking and trying not to pay attention to whatever disturbance was going on, the shouting became clearer and it became apparent these were two vendors who were arguing with one of the organizers of the street fair. Their issue was that their booths were located next to each other and that just was not acceptable to either one of them.

They were both in the business of selling incense, candles and various statuettes of various religious entities. However the concern was not with the competition, it was that they could not agree on religion.

Yet, both of these individuals very loudly professed to be extremely spiritual people. Eventually the situation was resolved when one of the vendors accepted a different spot a few booths down from the other.

Seriously though, here were two supposed business people, selling items of a spiritual nature, loudly yelling at each other about which one of them was actually more spiritual. I still find this amazing.

In my opinion, spirituality is a never-ending journey during which we do our very best to live our lives in the most loving possible way, and are completely non-judgmental and accepting of everyone else's path.

Spirituality is not the same as religion, some of the most spiritual people I've ever known do not belong to an organized religion at all. Spirituality is recognizing that we are all connected to each other and to the source and therefore, we each have a distinct purpose we are here to fulfill.

Our personal journey with whatever higher power we believe in, our continuing growth in our relationship with that higher power as well as all living beings and the development and continuing growth of our inner self and our ability to tap into the universal consciousness are all a part of our spirituality.

If you are always striving to be at peace within yourself and with everyone else; if you have an inner knowing that you are walking on your true path and if you live your life in a state of love and light, you are walking a spiritual path.

There is no street sign or secret handshake and you might not really think you feel any different at all. But there is an inner knowledge that you are on track, an inner calm that once you really allow yourself to acknowledge and feel it you know you will never be the same.

You might wonder why you should want to walk a spiritual path, and the short answer is that you are the best version of "you" when your body, mind and soul are in balance. Since you do live in this world, of course it is important to keep your body in the best possible working condition and most of us don't even think twice about doing things that will assist us in doing that. We exercise, we eat healthy and take vitamins or other supplements and see a doctor when we know there is something wrong that needs to be addressed; all of which greatly contribute to keeping us healthy.

Similarly, you strive to keep your mind sharp by reading, learning new things, meditating or maybe even by watching educational TV programs. However, we can often neglect nourishing our souls.

It's very easy to get caught up in work, getting ahead in life and in doing whatever we think we need to do in order to get those material things we think will make our lives perfect.

This is probably the reason so many very successful people turn to psychiatrists, psychologists and even the latest popular guru, so very often. They've come to realize that while they seemingly have everything, they've neglected to pay attention to their spiritual needs.

Many people get really confused and believe that you can't have material things as well as walk a spiritual path. This simply isn't true. In fact, there are very spiritual people who believe that since the universe is limitless and we are a part of the universe, it is the highest spiritual goal to achieve material things so that you can then help others.

Spirituality itself has really nothing to do with material stuff. True, if you're truly walking a spiritual path your priorities tend to change and those material things won't mean as much, but you can have both as long as you set your priorities and keep your balance. You need only take a look at the numerous charities that have been set up by very wealthy people to realize you can be both wealthy and spiritual.

I know, you're probably saying something right now about how the real reason people set up these charities and make large contributions to non-profit organizations is because they want the tax break. And, for some people, that may be a contributing factor. However, for most people this isn't really the case, they usually have a deep need to help a cause that's near and dear to their hearts.

These people have discovered that it feels really good to do good for others. Have you ever done something for someone or given something to someone just because it feels good to do so? That good feeling? That is your soul smiling because you've done something out of love, and not simply to get something in return.

You don't have to give something expensive; it doesn't even have to cost you a penny to give something that has a huge impact on the life of someone else. You can volunteer to give your time at a shelter or at a benefit event, you can donate clothing or another item you no longer need but that someone else could use, you can even simply smile at someone who looks like they're having a really bad day.

All of these things lend themselves to putting your soul back into balance with your mind and body, and that my friend, in the simplest form, is spirituality.

A very simple explanation of the Law of Attraction

When I started writing this book, I really never thought I would include anything about the Law of Attraction because I just didn't think it fit into what I thought this book would ultimately be about.

But, since it seems like everyone is talking about the "law" and since I have studied it at length and, at least try, to live my life according to it, I changed my mind and decided to include at least a cursory look at it. Obviously, there have been many entire books devoted to the Law of Attraction, and this is not intended to be one of those books.

A story I've told often about the Law of Attraction actually occurred when I was a teenager and in high school. A boy I knew went out and stole a stereo out of a car one night and installed it into his own car. The next day he went all around the school telling everyone how very clever he was having figured out how to get a nice stereo for free and how funny he thought it would have been to have seen the look on the guy's face when he realized his new and very expensive stereo had been stolen.

Since this was just a classmate and not really a friend, I simply ignored him even though I really thought someone should tell him what an idiot he was and how lucky he had been that he hadn't been caught. For days he bragged about this thing he had done. In fact, he bragged about it right up until the morning he went outside of his house and got in his car only to find the stolen stereo had been stolen.

At that point, he certainly didn't think it was funny, nor did he find the person who stole the stereo from him clever in the slightest. Well, you can't say he didn't get back what he put out into the universe, can you?

In the simplest context, the Law of Attraction says that whatever you think about most is what will come into your life. This is simply 'like attracts like.' According to the Law of Attraction, we are all magnets, drawing to ourselves whatever it is that we think most about. So, if you are always thinking about those things you do not have, or what is wrong with your life, you will attract more of those things you do not want or feel are wrong into your life.

If you are always thinking about what you have and how wonderful your life is, you will attract more of those things you love and want into your life.

The Law of Attraction, in my mind, is just an extension of being grateful for what you have. In fact, most people who teach the Law of Attraction do teach how very important it is to be grateful while you are using the Law of Attraction to bring into your life those things you want.

While it is very easy to say, well, your life is the way it is because you have attracted those events, situations, people, jobs, whatever-else-is-on-your-list, most people have a very difficult time believing this to be true.

Have you ever heard the saying," you get back what you put out?" Or how about "what comes around goes around" or even "karma works?" All of these are about the Law of Attraction.

People in general don't want to think they've brought anything bad on themselves, they don't like to blame the victim and they often don't realize the very powerful tool they have inside their own heads, that tool being our brains, or even how to utilize that tool in the highest and best possible manner.

If you really want to delve into a deeper understanding of the Law of Attraction, please feel free to read books, listen to tapes, or even look on the internet and you will find volumes of information. If you only read this information and you don't want to study any further than this, that's fine, you will still be able to utilize the Law of Attraction in your own life, however rudimentary your knowledge of it will be.

I consider this is a very important subject to become adept in and it will most certainly change your life. What I will give you here is simply a basic understanding of how to use the Law of Attraction in your life and is in no way to be considered everything you will want to, or should want to, know about the subject.

One way of working with the Law of Attraction is to write down exactly what you want in your life. What is that one huge thing that will make all the difference? Is that a new job or a new career? Maybe it's a new car or a new place to live.

Whatever that is for you is what you need to write down. Be as detailed as you can and really think as you're writing. Really and truly it doesn't make a huge difference what you write on your list, as long as you've spent some time thinking about what it really is that you want.

Once you have your first item on your list, you can either add something else or work with one thing at a time. Look at this list as often as possible and involve you emotions as much as you can.

Sometimes people will say "I don't know what I really want, but I sure know what I don't want." If this is you, write two lists.

In the first column write a list of those things you definitely do not want in your life. Directly across from that list add a second column and title that list things you do want. Let's say the first item on your list is that you don't want any more bills.

Ok, so immediately across from that item, write "all my bills are easily paid every month." See? You really DO know what you want; you've just allowed negative programming to take over your life to the point where you actually think about those things you don't want more than what you do want.

From this example I'm sure you can come up with many more items to put on both of your lists.

I have found the most effective way of utilizing the Law of Attraction personally is to combine it with meditation and visualization. Find a comfortable spot where you won't be disturbed, sit quietly and relax your thoughts, take some deep breaths and when you feel your mind is ready, form a mental image of what you want to manifest in your life.

Make this image as real and detailed as you can and hold it for several minutes. If you are able to, see yourself in this image, having whatever it is you want. If you are still having trouble constructing these images in your head, please keep working on it as you'll find it does help tremendously.

For example, if you really want a new home, see what that home looks like, walk through it, see the kitchen, see the bathrooms, see the bedrooms, the yards etc. Then, see yourself walking through the house in your mental image.

Of course, as with visualization, please be kind to yourself and realize you will feel most comfortable if you start with smaller goals and progress to larger ones as you become more accepting that you are as capable and deserving of manifesting larger goals as the smaller ones.

I like to spend as much time as I'm comfortable with in this state. Each meditation or visualization will likely be very different for you and you will intuitively feel when it's time to move onto the next step.

Whenever you're ready to move on, really feel what it is like to have this thing in your image. Let your emotions come to the surface. What are you feeling? Do you feel proud that you've been able to own this house? Are you excited about this new aspect of your life? Do you love the way your family is proud of you for this accomplishment? Spend several minutes getting in touch with your emotions about this image.

Feel as though this has already come to pass and your image is truly your reality right now, in this moment. When you feel you've poured as much emotion as you possibly can at this time into your image, come back to reality.

At this point, I always have people write a thank-you note to the universe, God, the Source, or whatever higher being you believe in. Just write down "Thank you for bringing (whatever your image was) into my life."

Allow yourself to believe, and feel, this is your reality right now and not in some future time. It is important to feel you are actually experiencing whatever you imagined as being your current truth.

Many people like to write down several things on a list, for example, you might write "I am so thankful I have the perfect job, I am so thankful I have a beautiful house, etc." Feel each thing on your list as if it has already entered your life, and be very grateful for this.

Your emotions are imperative in working with the Law of Attraction as that is what adds fuel to the fire of your subconscious mind and allows the universe to bring into your life those things you seek. Your emotions raise your personal energy vibrations to match those things you want to attract into your life. Like attracts like, remember?

Once you've done all this, you need to not obsess over your images. By obsessing over those things, you are actually reinforcing in your mind that these are things you do not have...therefore the universe will not bring them into your life because you are telling the universe you don't want them.

I know that sounds a bit backwards, because isn't the Law of Attraction basically saying that you get what you think about? Well, yes, that is why we tell people to emotionally feel what they want is already in their lives.

That's also why we say to express gratitude because those things are already in your life. You have to then let go of your attachment to how and when this is going to happen and just trust the universe.

You'll have to stay open to those opportunities that will undoubtedly present themselves to you. You have to stay grateful for both what you actually do have in your life now as well as those things you have instructed the universe to bring into your life, only do this while experiencing mentally and emotionally that you already have these things.

People, it seems, are not very patient. Many people try to work with the Law of Attraction once or twice and when their life does not change overnight, or they do not manifest anything immediately, they give up and say it doesn't work.

Like meditation, yoga or anything else, this takes some practice and dedication. You absolutely must feel you are worth the time to put in some time, effort and energy on the Law of Attraction for it to work. In fact, one of the first ways I used the Law of Attraction was to bring self-love, a sense that I deserved great things in my life and confidence into my life.

Truthfully, this was probably the most difficult manifestation I've done, but it did work. It is imperative that you not question the universe as to how or when things will come to you, because when you do this you are putting doubt into your mind. This takes some work. But, the Law of Attraction does work if you stick with it and learn to use it effectively and to the best of your ability.

The more you work with the Law of Attraction the better it works. I've known people who utilized the Law of Attraction for things as simple as finding a parking spot and as complex as finding the love of their life. Please keep in mind that if you truly are looking for the love of your life you can ask for specific attributes of the person you would like to find, but the Law of Attraction will not make a specific person fall in love with you.

Once you become competent with the Law of Attraction you will find it works faster and better for you. When you are just beginning, be prepared to spend more time than you think it will take and more effort than you originally thought you'd expend.

You have to learn to really trust in the universe, you have to truly be open to the possibilities and to opportunities that will show up almost magically. Of course, you still have to take advantage of these opportunities, but you will find they do show up for you to take advantage of. Learning and working with the Law of Attraction will be worth it in the end, and it does work for anyone who is willing to put in the effort.

Even if you find you aren't quite ready to dive in headfirst with the Law of Attraction, please at least take the time to write down your goals and dreams, think about them often, be grateful for those things you have and for everything you ever will have and concentrate on staying open to taking advantage of whatever opportunities come your way. These are all very easy things to do and will most certainly prove extremely beneficial to you along your life's path.

You're going to have some bad days

In spite of your best efforts, you're still going to have some really bad days! There's just no getting around it.

So, by this point in the book, you've probably begun learning to meditate, you've probably run across, or made your own, affirmations, you've been visualizing those things you really want in your life and you are well on your way to building confidence and getting your fear issues under control.

Maybe you've even thought about expanding your horizons and have decided to do something like take a class, apply for a different job or talk to that someone you've always meant to strike up a conversation with. First of all, that is wonderful!

Doing anything that, however briefly, takes you a bit out of your normal comfort zone will go a long way to producing a more positive and enriching life. These are things we must continue to do to as we keep on growing, learning and living. But, you have to be ever-mindful that not everyone will share your enthusiasm and not everything you undertake will be successful.

I think this is actually when many people give up - it isn't when they are feeling their most desperate and depressing emotions, it's after they've come through what they think is the worst part only to be knocked back down one more time.

There is a Buddhist saying a friend of mine is fond of saying, "our greatest glory is not in never falling, but in rising every time we fall." Just remembering that not everything is always going to turn out exactly the way you've envisioned will help to minimize the feelings of disappointment you may run into from time to time.

And, no matter how badly you feel something went, the truth is that it probably didn't really go that bad.

There is always something positive to take away from any situation, if you only look for it. Most of the time, there are actually a great many more positive things than there are negative ones.

A friend of mine was horrified after having what he considered to be a really bad day, he had just been studying the Law of Attraction and became convinced that he'd just sabotaged himself and undid everything positive he had been working on simply because he'd had such a bad day it was all he could think about.

His point was that if what we think about is what we really attract to ourselves, he was attracting a whole lot more really bad days. Everyone has bad days and some of them are really so bad it takes us some time to process, but this doesn't mean that you should give up and accept the fact that you are going to be attracting bad days for the rest of your life.

If you've been really concentrating on being positive and you really try to find something, anything really, that went well or that could be a learning experience that happened during your bad day you can really undo a lot of negative thinking. Just replace thinking about the really bad day you just had with thinking about a really good day you've had.

If there was a lesson to be learned, accept the lesson, learn it and tell the universe that you've got that one and don't need to learn it again. Just start being positive again the next day and move forward do not stay stuck in a bad day. I know I've said this before, but it is well worth repeating.

The first time I put together a poker-run benefit, which was something I had never done before even though I had done other types of fundraisers, I worked very hard at doing what I thought were all the right things...I passed out and pinned up hundreds of flyers, sent out invitations to those groups and clubs I thought would have an interest in participating, got many local businesses to donate raffle prizes, sent out about a hundred press releases to every newspaper, radio and TV station I could find, and had businesses put up banners advertising the event.

Since this was a motorcycle poker-run event, I also had to coordinate different stops along the ride where riders could draw their cards, stretch their legs and have access to food, water, and gasoline if needed.

Basically, I spent over a month completely throwing myself into this event and promoting it in every way I could think of to promote it. Still, this event did not go the way I had planned.

Almost immediately after the first flyers went out I received a very rude phone call from someone I had previously thought would be a very enthusiastic participant. This person simply did not approve of one of the stops along the route and proceeded to pretty much throw a fit about it, eventually refusing to participate at all.

Even after it was explained that this place was the only one available at that time on that day, this person still was not satisfied. Furthermore, this individual decided to let everyone they knew know exactly how unsatisfied they were by apparently telling other people not to participate.

Wow, how very unhappy do you really have to be in order to go to this extreme over something that is a benefit? This was only the most extreme thing we encountered while putting this event together.

As the day drew near we were informed that a number of other motorcycle rides were taking place in the very same area. This sort of surprised me because I knew we had contacted those very clubs and groups when we first began planning for this event.

Yes, it would have been nice if they had let us know they had a ride scheduled for that same day; or if they didn't have one scheduled then, it sure would have been a nice gesture if they'd picked a different day.

Oh well, we were already committed to that day by that time and decided to just make the best of it, no matter how it turned out. Personally I still felt we would be able to at least get a few people to show up, I convinced myself and most of the few others involved, to think positively.

The morning of the event was initially very disappointing though. In fact, if you looked at only the number of people who actually showed up to participate, this event would have been considered a failure. However, because of the amount of promotion I had done, I received a number of monetary donations from people who knew they would not be able to attend. Because of the number of raffle donations I received from local businesses, the money we raised actually at the event exceeded what I had realistically expected to raise from the raffle.

Best of all, the few people who did actually show up to attend the event turned out to be very well-connected and experienced event planners interested in assisting with future events! When the final dollar amounts were totaled, we actually met the monetary goal we had originally set for the event as well. So, while at first the event looked dismal, it was actually a resounding success!

Of course, many lessons were learned from this experience as well. I learned initially that the local people I had really thought would turn out because there just weren't ever events of this type in this area simply did not care about our event or the charity we were trying to raise money for.

Now, I know why other charities do not try and center fundraisers around this very beautiful, but remote, area. People who helped me with this event learned, right along with me, that in order to have a larger turn-out it is necessary to plan and promote longer than simply a bit over a month.

Friendships were formed and cemented during this experience; local businesspeople who had not even previously met began strategizing about how they could help each other. Most importantly, to me, is to learn the lesson that even if you try to do something good simply because it's the right thing to do, there are many people who will still be negative. Those people do not matter.

I included this story here because I want you to understand that there will always be people who just want to be negative, there will always be things that happen to you when you really didn't expect them and nothing is ever as easy as it seems to be when you first start out. That's just the way it is.

What will make you ultimately succeed when others might fail is the way you decide to look at these situations. Always look for the good, always learn the lesson and always congratulate yourself for doing something new, or different, or something that stretched your abilities and took you out of your comfort zone.

I look back on this event now with a great sense of pride and accomplishment. My very-small band of friends and I set out to do something simply because we felt it was the right thing to do, we had no idea how it would work out because we hadn't ever done anything quite like this before, but, we did it anyway.

That's the point. If you get an idea to do something for no other reason at all besides you just feel like it needs to be done, and you're doing this thing out of love and kindness for someone other than yourself. You need to do that thing.

I believe when we get these feelings to act, they are messages from our very souls saying "hey, here's what you need to do." Be grateful you have received the message; and don't forget to write thank-you cards to everyone who helps you along the way!

Childhood Trauma

I've mentioned my particular family many times throughout this book and I've talked about how sometimes they will be critical of you if you try to do anything different from the way you were raised, or the way they think you should live your life. However, dealing with families is such an intense emotional experience I decided to devote a bit more to this subject here.

Please, understand that these words could apply equally well to your current or past situations with your friends, spouse, children or whatever other people are in your life at present or at some other time in your adult life, as to the family you grew up with.

It's well known that most women grow up having issues with their mothers and most sons grow up with some conflicts with their fathers. This is simply a part of growing up. However, when these issues and conflicts turn particularly nasty and cause deep emotional wounds lasting well into the adulthood of the child, well, that isn't really a normal part of growing up.

Unfortunately, there are many adults today walking around with very deep wounds they suffered in childhood at the hands of their parents or other family members or both.

So, you've had a troubled childhood and you've just discovered this is a big part of the reason you've struggled as an adult...what do you do now? How do you even start healing a wound that's decades old? Many people turn to professional help and that's certainly a great decision if you feel that will help you.

Many other people don't have this option either because they don't have the money, don't have insurance to cover this, or don't live in an area where this type of help is available for free or all of the above. If you have found yourself in this situation, don't feel like you're just going to have to carry around all this old emotional trash for the rest of your life simply because you can't find professional help. You can do a lot of healing all on your own. Probably even all of the healing you need.

As I've said in other parts of this book, realizing the source of your emotional trash is the first step. Realizing that the source of your emotional trash is actually a parent is a very difficult realization to come to and sometimes this realization causes an additional source of trauma.

You may find yourself thinking, "why did I have this experience as a child?" or "why didn't I have parents who protected and loved me like other people?" You might even find feelings of guilt or even feelings of shame coming to the surface as you think back on your childhood.

Any feelings you find yourself experiencing are the feelings you need to allow to surface so you can deal with them and let them go. As an adult you can look probably back and maybe see the stress and unhappiness your parents were dealing with at the time. You may very well even be able to identify with them as they were at that time. Don't let that make you feel guilty for feeling how you felt as a child in that situation. Still, you do need to forgive the situation so that you can move forward without that particular trash.

This is a very difficult thing to come to grips with and it will probably take some time for you to untangle all the emotional wounds of your childhood, but you can do it. See if you can remember vividly one particular incident from your childhood that was especially painful. See yourself as that child. How old were you? What time of year was it? Where did you live? Remember as much detail about this situation as you possibly can and take as much time as you need to do so.

When you can feel you are right back at that place and time look at your younger self. Make eye contact with your younger self. Say to your younger self "I know it's hard right now, but you will survive this, life gets better and I love you." Do this at least three times and really mean it, it has to come right from your heart.

Some people actually visualize hugging their younger selves and this seems to help intensify the emotional connection you really need to make with the child you were in that situation in order to heal it and move forward without that baggage from your past. If you can do this, it is well worth your effort to do so.

Once you feel like you have completed this process, and again, please take as long as you need, tell the universe or whatever higher power you personally believe in that you are now ready to let this situation go completely. I like to visualize a balloon filling with all the pain from the situation and watch it floating away to be dissolved by the universal love and light.

You could also write down a detailed description of whatever happened and then burn the paper, safely of course. You could also do a more elaborate ritual where you burn a candle that represents this particular trauma, stating that as the candle burns it burns away that past pain.

I know of one person who goes to the ocean and throws rocks into the water, stating that the rocks symbolize the pain of the past and that the ocean absorbs and clears the negative energy associated with that pain. Any body of water would work well for this; you wouldn't have to make a special trip to the beach. Although, many people will tell you the ocean is extremely healing!

Of course, you can use whatever method you feel will work for you, if you meditate on it, I'm sure you can even come up with your very own method.

Understand that these deep wounds from childhood are unlike those you've encountered later in your life as an adult simply because as children we feel we should be loved and nurtured and not neglected, ignored and/or abused.

Therefore, you may actually have to go through this ritual with each and every dark memory you find yourself starting to remember from that time in your early life. This is actually a very good thing; it means you are uncovering more and more painful trash that you can take out. Stick with it and you'll find you're feeling better and better, maybe even better than you ever remember feeling.

Recovering from the death of a loved one

You might think this topic really doesn't belong in this book. And, who knows, you might be right. I have included it because it was the very much unexpected death of a very close friend that provided the push I needed to actually sit down and write this book. The book I've literally started and stopped at least a dozen times over the past couple of decades.

As the result of this death, the thought that I might run out of time and actually never write this book occurred to me, and the pain of that thought was greater than my fear of actually doing it. That is the reason for this subject being included. I hope you will understand.

The death of a loved one is always difficult and often devastating. Too often, there are so many people around immediately after the loss it is difficult to begin the grieving process.

Sometimes, these days are so filled with people trying to force themselves to find something to be happy about it feels more like a party than a gathering because someone died. Then, all of a sudden, everyone is gone and we are left to our own devices.

Many people feel like they are jolted by the loss all over again at this point and don't know what to do or where to turn. It is important to let yourself feel what you feel, openly and unabashedly, no matter what those feelings might be.

Only by letting yourself feel the pain, the anger, the relief, the sorrow or whatever other emotions surface, will you be able to truly grieve your loss and begin to see a life without the deceased.

Many people feel a sense of guilt that they are still alive and their loved one is not. Sometimes people feel guilty due to the erroneous feeling that they should have said or done something that would have prevented the death or eased the deceased's suffering. Or, they will experience feeling guilty for realizing they are actually angry at the deceased for dying and leaving them.

Please remember, whatever emotions you feel are the correct emotions for you to be feeling at that time. During the grieving process you will have "good" days and "bad" days.

Do not feel bad for feeling bad, but congratulate yourself on those days you are able to see past your grief, even if it's only for just a minute or two. Like any other journey, the journey through grief takes time, patience with yourself, and baby steps to make it through.

You're going to fall, get back up and fall down again. You're going to stumble and probably curse and get angry and be sad so many times you will get to the point where you really aren't completely sure what you're feeling. But, you will make it through.

Don't ever confuse "surviving grief" with "you stop missing them" it's been 20 years since my grandmother died and I still do miss her every day. We were very close, and I really believe she is the reason I actually survived many of my darkest moments and she's the reason I've achieved anything positive at all in my life.

It might seem difficult for some people to believe, but on the night she died she came and told me goodbye and that she had to leave. This would not be surprising unless you consider we were about 1800 miles apart that night. That was only time I ever fought with her and I was yelling at her to 'get back here' and 'you're not going anywhere.' Yet, I was actually asleep. I woke up the next morning fully expecting the phone call that came shortly after I woke up. It was intense to say the least.

So many people think they will be able to prepare for the inevitable death of a loved one. Please understand that you will never be completely prepared. I think that's because our souls know they never really leave us.

Personally, I have found it has helped me to talk to my deceased loved ones for days or longer after they had passed. There are times when I still find myself talking to my grandmother. If you open your heart, you will realize they are still there for you, just in a different form.

Sometimes I will talk to them as if they were still alive, literally talking about the weather and how my garden is doing, the silly thing my daughter said or did, what I am making for dinner and so on.

Other times I will just tell them how much I miss them and how very much I love them. For most of the time though, I just talk about things I remember; both the good and bad.

As long as we hold on to one memory about them, whether it is a loving memory, a funny memory or even a moment we wish we could have taken back, they will always be a part of our life and our heart.

So, even though their body is gone, we are never truly without them. Everyone you've ever loved is a part of your very essence and has made you who you are today.

Very often those who have lost a very close loved one will experience severe bouts of guilt associated with the loss. It is very common to say "if only I had done..." and while it's understandable, please know your loved one would not want you to take on this guilt.

If you feel you made your deceased loved one do something they would not have done without you and this lead to their death, please understand that if this is the case they would have done this purely out of love for you. Making you feel loved and happy is what made them feel loved and happy. Most likely however you could not really have "made" them do anything. Even if it was your idea and you strongly suggested over and over again that this was the thing to do; they ultimately made their own decision to go ahead with it.

Whether you are dealing with extreme stress, illness or guilt, your feelings are very real and deserve to be taken seriously. You must be kind to yourself, give yourself the space and time you need to feel those feelings, fully process your feelings, and even embrace those feelings. Only after this can you really deal with these feelings and let them go. Remember that your love for your loved one will never go away they will always be a part of you. They want you to be able to move forward with your life and to be happy again.

Above all, when you think you can't possibly go on...give it one more try, one more day, even just one more hour. At some point, those hours, days and tries start combining and you come to realize that you have, in fact, gone on.

When you come to this realization, give yourself a hug, a special treat and very large congratulations! Don't ever underestimate the strength it has taken you to actually move through a very difficult time.

Sometimes the deaths we have the most difficulty handling is when the death is that of a pet rather than a person. With people, we pretty much know for certain how they feel about us, we are certain they know we love and care about them and there have probably even been discussions at various times about death and dying, and how they would want us to handle that situation. But, with an animal, well, most people just aren't sure of much at all.

I've been asked many times," do they love us, do they know we love them?"And so on. I can assure you, yes, they most certainly do love their people and they absolutely know we love them as well.

Of course, I think anyone who has ever loved an animal can attest that when you look into their eyes, you truly do see completely unconditional love. Sometimes there is also fear, especially in the case of an abused animal. But, look again, with an open heart and all you'll see is love.

Animals have the purest of souls and they don't hide their feelings like people do. So, when you have a special bond with an animal and that animal dies, your heart can grieve as much or even more than with the death of a very close person.

Years ago when I lost a very special dog, most people told me "it's just a dog, why are you so upset?' Now, most people realize the very special bonds that exist between us and our much beloved animal friends and they treat these deaths much like those of a person.

The steps in grieving the loss of a pet are the same as grieving the loss of a special person in your life, and you shouldn't let anyone deprive you or even try to deprive you of this process.

Often people will go out and get another pet and that's fine as long as you understand that animals, just like people, are all unique individuals and you cannot "replace" the one you lost with one that looks the same.

Other people need a long period of time to get over the loss before even thinking about another pet, and that's fine as well. In my case, usually my next pet finds me without my even having to look. When my family's Corgi, Bandit, (also known as the best dog ever) died my husband and I talked about getting another dog.

But, at the time we also had an older Great Pyrenees who was beginning to have trouble patrolling our farm at night. We decided not to try and find another Corgi at that point because, well let's face it, Corgi's are not exactly livestock guard dog material. We happened to be at some friends' house for dinner and were talking about dogs since it was shortly after Bandit had died and they had known him.

About two or three days later one of these friends called me and asked if I was at home because she needed to come by with something for me. Sure enough, someone had dropped off puppies near their house and they had decided one of them was ours. Now, I wouldn't recommend doing this to your friends because it might not be as well received as it was by us. But, these friends know us well and knew exactly what type of dog would fit into our lives.

No matter how you grieve the loss of an animal companion, it's the right way for you to grieve. Don't let anyone tell you you're doing something wrong.

Death is a part of life and there's just no way to get around it, so take care of yourself, feel whatever emotions you feel, and do whatever you need to do in order to move through your grief and rejoin your life already in progress.

While most of us can certainly identify with either the death of a loved person or animal in our lives, I've recently encountered a situation that I had not personally considered before.

A friend came to me with her young child who was terribly distraught over a particular tree that was cut down during a road-widening project. I have to admit, while I've been upset in the past by similar situations, I did not become absolutely distraught as this child had become from the destruction of a tree and I wasn't sure exactly what to tell her about comforting this child.

The sensitivity of this particular child truly touched me and I saw a great resemblance between this little person and myself at around the same age. After talking for a while we determined that a tree funeral or memorial was definitely in order.

I found out later they had gone and retrieved some of the broken branches that remained on the ground from the tree, took them home and glued them together to form a sort of square wreath they hung on their front door. Originally they had talked about burying these branches, but decided making something they could look at every day that would remind them how wonderful the tree had been seemed like a more fitting tribute.

Really I suppose the main point here is that our hearts know what they truly love and sometimes what that is won't make sense to everyone. And, that is ok. This is just one more example of how wonderful our differences are and yet how very similar we are at the same time. Grief is a part of being human; death is a part of life. How we grieve and what we grieve over are often very personal experiences, yet at the same time we share these experiences with everyone.

Introduction to Part Two

The first part of this book has been about making yourself feel better, healing old wounds however you need to heal them and getting back to what I call "ground level." You've come up out of a deep dark place and have rejoined your life already in progress.

You've undoubtedly uncovered some very unpleasant memories along the way and hopefully have uncovered some very long-forgotten, but very happy ones as well.

It is my sincerest hope you are feeling much better and have come to a sort of awakening within yourself with regards to your true path in life and with your spirituality.

The second part of this book deals with questions commonly discussed among myself, my clients and others who have walked through the fire and have come through the other side.

If you've been meditating and have made progress along your spiritual path, you have probably begun noticing things you may not have always believed in.

For example, you might catch a glimpse of something out of the corner of your eye, you might see occasional orbs and you may find you have moments of "knowing" something you have no way of knowing.

If this is happening to you, congratulations! If it isn't yet, don't give up because most likely it will as long as you want these experiences and are open to them.

Energy Work

Energy is all around us, it is everywhere and in everything, including ourselves. There different ways to work with this energy, but in each there is the acceptance that this energy is universal in nature.

We need only tap into it. Most people who perform energy work believe we were all born with this ability, but through our lives this ability has gone dormant. We've simply forgotten about it altogether.

Some energy workers believe this energy is spirit in nature, others believe it is a connection with the divine but no matter what their personal beliefs regarding its origin, it is generally agreed this energy is a very powerful and healing force that is much-needed in today's world.

In Reiki, and many other forms of energy work, the energy is concentrated around points in our bodies called chakras. While there are actually many chakra centers, there are seven primary points most people concentrate on. If you have an energy blockage in one or more chakras, you will not feel as well as you could and things will not be going quite as well as you think they should be in general.

You can actually feel this energy yourself. Hold your hands about six or so inches apart with your palms facing each other. After several seconds you should be able to feel a sensation between your hands. If you can't, try again with your hands closer together. Your hands will probably begin to get warm, or even hot. This is the universal energy.

Reiki practitioners tap into this energy and utilize it to send waves of positive energy through a person's chakras in order to heal them. Actually you don't even need to be actually sick for this to help you, everyone carries around negativity in one form or another and this energy can clear it before it begins to be bothersome.

Keep in mind that the practitioner does not generate this energy through themselves; they are merely the channel through which this energy flows.

You actually already have this same ability within yourself, if you could feel the energy between your hands, you can use this energy to heal yourself or at least make yourself feel better. If you want to try this, visualize a bright white light surrounding you, this will keep negative energies away from you while you are working with positive energy.

Let's say you've had a headache for a while and it just won't go away completely. What I do is first feel the energy between my hands as we've done earlier, then I move that energy up to my head where it hurts. You can use one or both hands. It may help you to visualize a bright light penetrating your head and dissolving the headache.

If you concentrate as you do this exercise you will be successful, and I personally have had success with this time and time again; not only with headaches, but with sprains or sore muscles and even upset stomachs.

Of course, this technique is not really "Reiki" but it works in much the same way. You don't have to embark on a study of Reiki, or any other energy healing technique, in order to make use of this energy that's all around us. However, I would recommend you at least learn the seven main chakra points simply so you can more effectively heal your own life. So, what are these main chakra points and what do they do?

The first primary chakra people work with is the Root Chakra and it is located in your pelvic area, and some people actually locate this "root" at the base of our spines.

I normally visualize the Root Chakra as being a red ball that is large enough to encompass the entire area from the front of your pelvis to your lower back, including the base of your spine. Each chakra has a color associated with it and the color for the Root Chakra, as I mentioned, is red.

Likewise, each chakra has a specific set of properties associated to it and the properties associated to the Root Chakra are physical in nature. This is the grounding chakra and it connects us to the earth and our sense of belonging. If we are feeling out of balance, insecure or like our physical needs are not being met we may very well have a blockage in our Root Chakra.

Money issues are also associated with this chakra and if you are experiencing money problems they may be due, at least in part, by a blockage in your Root Chakra. If you've never been particularly fond of the color red and all of a sudden you're seeing red everywhere, or you're experiencing a desire to go out and buy something red, you may have a Rood Chakra blockage and your inner voice is telling you to take care of it. I have personally found this to be the case in the past when I've worried about money.

There are many different ways to clear a blockage in the Root Chakra, but if I'm feeling particularly not grounded I like to place both hands on the top of my head and jump. Yes, seriously. This has the effect of reattaching me to the earth and really does seem to ground me. Meditating on clearing this chakra is extremely effective as well and I like to visualize a bright red light in the area of my Root Chakra getting clearer and brighter as it clears away any blockages I have.

The second primary chakra people work with is the Sacral Chakra, located about a couple of inches below your belly button. This chakra corresponds to your emotional state, sexuality and creativity and the color associated with this chakra is orange.

If you've ever experienced a time when you felt particularly "needy" like you just couldn't get enough reassurance and someone actually accused you of being clingy you've experienced an out of balance and blocked Sacral Chakra. In my experience, people have more blockages in this chakra than in any other. A blockage in this chakra can cause negative emotions such as anger, depression and guilt; other issues such as obsessions, addictions or even health issues such as kidney stones other urinary issues and lower back pain.

Many times people with a blockage in their Sacral Chakra will experience the same type of negative things over and over again simply because this chakra acts as a magnet, drawing in more of whatever is already there.

To balance the Sacral Chakra, I like to use a combination of things. First off, I like to wear something orange and I find that simply noticing the orange color I can start to feel a balancing affect.

Secondly, exercise or dance, especially a physical activity that involves your mid-section, is very helpful in balancing this chakra. One really fun activity that I've heard people do is hula-hooping. This has the added benefit of making people feel silly and stop taking themselves so seriously.

Meditating on a large orange ball getting brighter and clearer is also a very good way to balance the Sacral Chakra; and many people even like to eat orange foods or bring orange flowers into their environment. The Sacral Chakra is also associated with water, so swimming or even simply taking a bath are also good ways to bring this chakra into balance.

The third primary chakra is the Solar Plexus Chakra. This chakra corresponds to our intellect, self-esteem, personal power and ego. It is located at the point where your ribs come together, between your navel and your ribs. The color for this chakra is yellow.

If you find yourself overly anxious, doubting every decision you make and/or avoiding your feelings completely you probably can trace this right back to a blockage of your Solar Plexus. Blockages of the Solar Plexus can manifest into weight issues, both over and under weight, ulcers, other digestive issues and even arthritis. In some cases it is thought severe mental issues can also be linked to a blockage in this chakra.

So, how do you heal the Solar Plexus Chakra? Again, use of the associated color, in this instance yellow, has been shown to begin the process of clearing a blocked chakra.

Whether you decide to eat yellow foods, wear yellow clothing, burn yellow candles or simply go outside and enjoy the yellow sunshine, incorporating this color will certainly help clear any blockages in your Solar Plexus Chakra. Much like in the case of the Sacral Chakra, physical activity is also recommended as is meditation.

One person I know makes it a habit to meditate on clearing blockages in this area daily and she does this by visualizing a bright yellow light surrounding her then slowly moving into her Solar Plexus Chakra until it is completely absorbed. Pick a method or several that seem to resonate with you.

The fourth chakra we're going to go into here is the Heart Chakra. This chakra is located, where you might imagine it would be, in the center of your chest. The color associated with the Heart Chakra is green, and this chakra not only is associated with love and relationships but also with personal values, ethics and self discipline.

If you feel excessively lonely, are experiencing a sense of being alienated from friends and/or family or a lack of self-discipline, it's likely you have a blockage in your Heart Chakra.

Getting outside and into fresh air and nature is probably the most beneficial thing I've ever found for balancing the Heart Chakra. Of course, you can also use the color-therapy method whereby you bring the color green into your life whether you eat green foods, wear green clothing, burn green candles, etc.

You can also meditate, surrounding yourself with a bright green light or simply meditate on love and the sense of well-being. Some people use affirmations such as "I am love" or "I am at peace" and others find seeking out and spending time with old friends, children and/or animals give them the sense of balance to their Heart Chakra they've been missing.

As always, intent it key, so whatever method you decide to try make sure you hold your desire to heal your Heart Chakra firmly in your mind.

The Throat Chakra is the fifth primary chakra and it is located at the base of your throat in the center of your collarbone. As you might expect, the Throat Chakra is associated with our voice, our truth and how we express ourselves and our truth to others.

The color for the Throat Chakra is light blue, and if you are experiencing issues with this chakra you are probably having difficulty in being completely honest or with being misunderstood or you could also become overly opinionated and critical. Many times a blockage in your Throat Chakra can lead to throat abscesses, problems with teeth or even earaches and sinus issues. You might even find you are having pain in your neck and/or shoulders.

As with healing the Heart Chakra, I have personally found that going outside is extremely helpful in healing the Throat Chakra. I like to sit outside or lie on the grass and look up at the blue sky and visualize the sky helping to clear away any blockages in my Throat Chakra that are keeping me from freely speaking my truth. You can also wear blue, or otherwise incorporate the color of light blue into your day. I know several people who like to sing or chant to balance their Throat Chakra and meditating on a bright sky blue light will also work.

If you have been feeling disoriented, have been prone to daydreaming more than usual or have been experiencing difficulty sleeping you might be having issues with your Third Eye Chakra. This chakra is, of course, associated with our conscious and subconscious mind and intuition, and is located between and slightly above our eyes; almost in the center of your forehead.

When this chakra is working as it should be, we experience mental acuity, intuition and focus. We care about others and feel healthy and as though everything is right with the world. The Third Eye Chakra is the sixth of the primary chakras.

The color for the Third Eye Chakra is an indigo or dark purple-blue and while I routinely add this color to my wardrobe when I feel the need to add energy to my Third Eye Chakra, I have found the very best method of clearing blockage from this chakra is meditation.

You can do a meditation with the intent of opening your third eye, you can meditate on clearing this chakra or you can meditate while visualizing a bright indigo light enveloping you then being absorbed into your Third Eye Chakra.

Of course you could also burn dark blue or purple-blue candles or add this color to your day in any other way you choose to do so. Many people also practice either Sun or Moon gazing as a way to clear blocks from their Third Eye Chakra.

I can tell you I personally love to just go outside and stare at the moon, and it does most certainly seem to help with my Third Eye Chakra; but, I would not recommend you go out and try to stare at the sun. This is an extremely dangerous thing to do under the best of circumstances, and especially when you don't really have a clue as to how Sun Gazing is really practiced. Leave this method to those who really understand what they're doing. Please.

The seventh primary charka is associated with the color purple or violet and some people even use the color white when working with the Crown Chakra. This chakra is at the top of your head and sometimes you'll see this chakra represented with a lotus flower.

Connecting us to our spirituality and the collective consciousness of the universe as a whole is the primary attribute associated with the Crown Chakra. When you have a blockage or other issue with your Crown Chakra you are likely uninspired, confused or over-thinking everything. You might feel as though you've lost your spirituality or even your connection to yourself.

By far the most effective way to clear blockages from your Crown Chakra and restore balance is meditation. Whether you visualize a bright violet or white light, or you choose affirmations to concentrate on or you simply sit in a quiet meditation doesn't really matter.

The Crown Chakra is the center of our spirituality and meditation truly is the best way to reconnect to your spirituality. Some people ask their spirit guides, angels or elementals to assist them, but I've found simply meditating for a while works well.

There is a wealth of material on chakras widely available and it is well worth your time, if you are so inclined, to do some research in this area. Many people I know use color therapy in working with chakra blockages and I have found this to be probably the easiest method of balancing and clearing chakra energy.

You will find you can incorporate crystals, incense, music and many other things into your energy work or you can come up with something completely different that resonates with you. The common thread is to be open and to allow yourself to feel this energy; you'll certainly recognize it when it happens for you.

What about working with crystals?

Many people use crystals in the colors that correspond to the chakra they are working with and that is a great thing if you are thinking about doing this. Understand though, that this isn't really necessary at all, you can visualize whatever color you need to assist you in energy work.

Crystals do, however, have their own energies and many people feel pulled toward certain ones or several ones. If you find yourself wanting to work with crystals, here are what I think are the best ones to start working with, in no particular order. These are simply the ones I think are easiest to find and are most suited to those who are just starting out with crystals.

When you do get your crystals, no matter which one or ones you decide on, you will need to cleanse them of any energy they may have picked up from someone else. There are many ways of doing this, but I prefer simply placing them in a container of water in the moonlight and leaving them there until morning. You can either do this outside or inside on a window sill, it will work either way.

The most obvious crystal and the most popular one by far is clear quartz. This is my all-purpose, go-to crystal for any number of things as clear quartz simply amplifies energy and acts as an energy transmitter. Clear quartz resonates with all of the chakras, so is a terrific balancing and healing crystal as well. If you can only get a single crystal, I think this is the one to have.

Amethyst is a beautiful purple crystal and one you often see in geode form. I love amethyst for its ability to raise your vibration and because it helps development of the third eye. Most people on a spiritual journey gravitate to amethyst because of its usefulness with things of a spiritual nature. You can also use amethyst as a healing stone and it works especially well to combat grief and symptoms of depression or other emotional turmoil.

One of my favorite crystals personally is Rose Quartz. While mostly found as a tumbled crystal rather than in point form, rose quartz is very well suited to carrying around in a pocket when you're feeling emotionally drained or upset. Rose quartz is closely associated with affairs of the heart and has a very loving, calming energy about it. Most people find rose quartz especially soothing and find it enhances their ability to feel compassion and love for others as well as themselves.

Aventurine is very similar to rose quartz in that it is also associated closely to the heart. However, aventurine is a light green crystal and is more often used to protect against negativity of the heart rather than to heal the heart after it has already been wounded.

Lapis Lazuli is a beautiful dark blue crystal with gold and white flecks, and I've seen some with grayish flecks as well. Lapis is a great crystal to use when you're trying to rid yourself of trash from your past as it helps to release old emotional pain as well as depression and anxiety caused by holding on to those old ties. Many people also use Lapis to aid in astral travel and psychic development.

Agate comes in a variety of colors and is very good for promoting general happiness and good health. I do know people who say agate helps to promote fertility, prosperity and intelligence but I've never really worked with agate enough personally in those specific areas to give an opinion about such things. I do know agate has a very nice energy and is one stone I usually do have with me simply because I really like it.

In my opinion if you find yourself battling sad moods often, you would do very well to get yourself a citrine. Citrine is a very pretty yellow color and is known for the ability to bring happiness, wealth and prosperity. Being the color of the sun, citrine has a warm and vibrant energy and is well-suited to turning negative thoughts and feelings into positive ones. While many people will say citrine doesn't hold on to negativity at all so it never needs to be cleansed, I would err on the side of safety and do so anyway.

These are just a few of the amazing number of crystals you might want to work with, and just because someone uses their crystals for specific things doesn't mean you have to do what they do. Find the crystals that you like and open your heart and mind to hear how you might want or need to use them.

I know just as many people who use amethyst to heal emotional issues as I do who use rose quartz for the same type of trouble. There are other people who only use clear quartz and they use that crystal for every single type of healing or energy work they do.

If you listen to your inner voice you will hear what you need to know, don't necessarily do what anyone else tells you is the "right" thing to do or the "right" way to use a crystal.

There are no "crystal authorities" who will come in and tell you you're doing something wrong and it is no one else's business if you'd rather not use citrine because you really don't like the color yellow or if you've always found clear quartz boring so you'd rather use an agate.

Totem animals

Most people have at least one or two favorite animals they've loved throughout their lives and really never figured out why. It is easy to say I love dogs because I had a wonderful pet dog, or I've always loved cats because I grew up with them.

But, this isn't really what totem animals are about; while you might very well have cats or dogs as your totem animals most totem animals are not domestic animals at all. In fact, I know people who count animals like unicorns or phoenixes among their totem animals, so in their way of thinking, totem animals don't even have to be verified as being "real".

While totem animals are closely associated with Native American culture, truthfully this practice is common in many religions closely aligned with nature. As with spirit guides, angels and elementals there are different names depending on the specific culture or religion, but the basic premise is the same.

Our totem animals are our teachers, our protectors and our friends when we need them. Different animals can come and go throughout our lives, but normally there is one or two that stay with us always.

Most people have between five and nine totem animals at any given time, when an animal keeps appearing to you, whether during a meditation, a dream or even in life, they are trying to send you a message.

If you all of a sudden feel a particular affinity with a certain animal, again, that animal is trying to bring a message to you. Likewise, if you suddenly find yourself dreaming of a particular animal it's time to figure out what this animal is telling you.

At one time in my life I dreamt constantly of snakes, either a snake would be on my porch or in a tree or even simply suddenly appear right in front of as I walked in a dream. Sometimes they would be in the process of shedding their skin and other times they would just be there.

I finally got the message they were trying to give me. That message was that I should "shed my skin" and release old habits and pain and move forward along my life path with "new skin".

There is a wealth of information online about totem animals and their meanings and I encourage you to seek out information about the animals you feel particularly in tune with. I've included some of the most common here, but again, please do not think this is an exhaustive list.

You will find that if you are open to receiving, their messages will assist you greatly along your path; they will bring you encouragement, advice and warnings. Not everyone chooses to work with or even acknowledge their spirit or totem animals and that's fine too, they'll still be around just in case you change your mind.

One of the most common animals people feel a kinship with is the bear. The most common meaning associated with the bear is motherhood. It is well known bears are excellent and very protective mothers and will not hesitate to attack anything that gets too close to her babies.

Bears also represent strength, courage and power. Since bears also hibernate, if they are a recurring animal in your meditations or dreams it could be a message that you need to "hibernate" some of your plans or projects for a while until you are truly ready to proceed.

Another animal many people feel connected to is the wolf. Wolves signify loyalty, family, intelligence and compassion among other things. If you feel drawn to the wolf, you are probably are being sent a message pertaining to your friends and family or possibly even your relationship with yourself. Are you being open and honest with yourself? Are you being a loyal friend and are your friends being loyal to you? Is there a family member who is feeling as if you aren't there for them or is there a family member you are thinking isn't being honest with themselves or with others? Wolf is asking you to answer these questions and evaluate your answers.

Horses are a spirit or totem animal for many people and the horse symbolizes freedom and power.

Have you been feeling like you are "caged" or stuck in a situation? Personally when I've felt either stuck or caged in my life I've dreamed of horses, or have had the image of a horse pop into my head when meditating. This is a message to strive for balance in your life and to not get too caught up in a single area or on a single project. You always have the freedom and power to move forward, you just have to get out of your own way at times.

If you are drawn to the owl, you might be not seeing or noticing something that you really should be paying attention to. Or you may have recently reached a point on your path where you've suddenly realized you CAN see or intuit things you've never been able to before.

Owl is often associated with those who are either interested in or actually practicing magical arts such as shamanism or witchcraft, but don't let this dissuade you from connecting with the owl as the owl also symbolizes wisdom and the ability to see the truth.

Another feathered totem animal that many people feel connected to is the Hawk. Hawks usually indicate you need to be open to receiving a message that life and the universe are sending you signals you should be paying attention to.

The hawk tells us to be observant and to look at the entire situation and examine things from a higher perspective. Once you've taken in the whole situation you can then decide which direction you need to go in and on what details you need to zoom in on.

Ravens are probably one of the most misunderstood and maligned of total animals because of their black color. However, the color black is only a color and is neither "good" nor "bad." Ravens have been associated with magic and mystery, but Raven is also a messenger and keeper of secrets.

If you've been feeling like you're in a rut, call on Raven to bring energy and a spiritual awakening into your life so that you will see the magic in everything. If you've recently told someone's secret or you've been wishing something bad would happen to someone else, Raven may very well come calling to let you know this is not the way to walk along a spiritual path and you need to refocus your energy on your personal growth.

The Frog is my absolute favorite totem animal and is the one I've kept my entire life. Frog symbolizes transformation and transition, which makes perfect sense as the frog goes from egg, to tadpole to frog.

If you are feeling drawn to Frog, you might be experiencing rapid changes in your life or that you are coming into your own personal power. Frog may also be sending you a message that a spiritual cleansing is needed to clear away negativity from the past so you can replenish your spirit.

The frog is closely associated with people who are empathic as frog energy enables people to be great listeners and to give well-thought-out and caring advice.

As I said earlier, if you are suddenly finding yourself drawn to or dreaming about or seeing snakes, you may be either embracing change or resisting change. Snakes shed their skin, and like the snake, you may be experiencing an awakening and shedding old patterns of thought or old habits or even old emotional wounds.

You will need to be conscious of staying true to yourself while you are undergoing this change and make sure your energy is clear, or you might end up in a very different situation than what you intended.

Turtles generally represent grounding and creativity and protection. The turtle teaches us to reconnect with the earth and to fully develop our ideas and plans fully before trying to manifest them.

Many people also associate turtles with financial abundance and with gratitude for everything in our lives. If you've been feeling especially disconnected or "spacey" you can ask turtle to help you become grounded again.

The butterfly teaches us about the beauty and lightness of life and about transformation. Each moment of our life can be viewed as begin in a state of change as we are never truly stagnant.

Every goal or dream you have is either at the beginning or egg stage, the decision or larval stage, the development or cocoon stage or at the completion or butterfly stage. Butterfly can give you a clearer picture of your mental process and can help you determine what your next step should be. If you find yourself resisting change or unable to move forward in a project, you can ask butterfly to help you find the courage to make the necessary changes.

Create, is the message of Spider, whose webs wove the first alphabet according to some Native American legends. If you find you are being drawn to spiders, you might be being sent a message that you've become impatient or you are getting too caught up in one aspect of your project and you're in danger of missing out on an opportunity. You may have to regain your perspective in order to really meet your goals.

Dragonfly tells us to keep the love and lightness in our lives, but at the same time to pay attention because things aren't always as they seem. Dragonfly is the illusionist and the harbinger of change. Follow your intuition and go your own way, don't try to do things anyone else's way and don't worry about proving your way is the right one to anyone else. It's your path remember that you alone create your own life.

Once you begin looking into totem and spirit animals you will find many, many others that will resonate with you personally and that is exactly the way it should be. You will also find that you will feel drawn to different animals at different times, and you are always free to ask for a certain animal spirit to come to you and be of assistance.

Different spirit animals have different energies and attributes and you will learn which ones to utilize at which times as you walk along your path. And, just because one person calls on a certain spirit or totem animal for a certain assistance, doesn't mean you have to use the same one for the same thing. Trust your intuition to guide you as to what you really need at any time.

Many people keep pictures or other representations of their favorite animals. I've known people who purchased candles in the shape of the animal whose attributes they wanted to invite into their lives and then they would meditate on those attributes while burning the candle.

There are many different ways of working with animal energy, just stay open to the possibilities and you will find ways of your own. As with anything else of a spiritual nature, you should always listen to your inner voice, it knows what you need.

And the qualities normally associated with certain animals may be very different from the qualities you personally associate with them. For example, my entire life I've loved frogs, to me, frogs symbolize endless possibilities and sensitivity. I also see beauty in snakes and bravery in butterflies. There really is no right or wrong here, if you feel drawn to an animal rest assured there is some quality in that animal you either have or need.

Plant "totems"

Besides working with crystals and animals, plants too have their own different energies and attributes. While not as much has been written about using plants as about using crystals and animals, you can still find a lot of information on this subject.

To find what plants you resonate with you only need to go outside and pay attention. I know that when I'm feeling off balance or weak I am drawn to tall, straight pine trees or to strong, unyielding oaks.

If I feel I need to be a bit more flexible in a situation, then I naturally gravitate to willow trees or even tall grass. Pay attention to your inner voice and you'll learn exactly what you need. Here are just a few examples, there are really endless possibilities.

The aforementioned Willow is considered a healing and protective tree and is the true source of modern-day aspirin. I've always loved the way willows will sway in the wind, yet remain standing and this is one attribute that makes many people gravitate towards this tree.

Oddly enough, grass also is considered healing and protective and I've often wondered if it isn't simply because tall grass blowing in the wind seems to me to be very similar to a willow tree blowing in the wind. Many people find watching tall grass in the wind to be very calming and soothing.

Many evergreen trees like pine, juniper and cedar are considered to be protective as well and their cones, bark and leaves are considered to be an effective way to eliminate negativity from any area.

Evergreen trees are also symbolic of the everlasting life of the soul because they do stay green even during the darkest, coldest winter. Many people also associate healing properties with these evergreen trees.

Just about every single plant has been or could be used for a different purpose, and even with the same plant, different people have used it for different purposes. The key is to find what speaks to you, what feels right for you.

Pay particular attention to colors of plants and especially flowers that you feel drawn to. Have you been feeling down and all of a sudden you realize you've felt better since you saw those bright yellow flowers? Have you found that blue violets are just the thing to clear your bad mood? If you start really being present in your life you'll start noticing all sorts of things.

Do what makes you feel good. I have found having fresh flowers on my table or desk keeps me more focused on the task at hand and makes me more productive. I know several people who find the very best stress reliever they know of is simply walking barefoot on a grassy lawn or walking barefoot on the beach.

Whether you incorporate trees, flowers, grass or animals or crystals into your meditation or even into your life, you will find the more you do for yourself that makes you feel good the higher your self-esteem will be and the more spiritual and free your life will feel. Eventually you'll come to realize you have very little trash left to take out.

Developing your psychic abilities

You've taken out your trash and now you want to develop your psychic abilities.

I'm not sure why, but probably the most common question I've gotten from clients who have finally taken out their emotional baggage and subconscious trash for good is about developing psychic abilities.

People want to be able to see auras, develop psychic abilities and become mediums once they become comfortable in their own skin. First off, I believe that everyone is born with all of these abilities; it's just that many people either turn these abilities off as young children or they just simply forget they ever existed.

Secondly, if we have the ability to turn these things off and/or forget they existed surely we have the ability to turn them back on and/or remember again.

I tell people who want to develop their psychic ability to simply let themselves believe they are psychic. As we've learned earlier in this book, positive affirmations work, so simply begin saying to yourself "I am psychic." Repeat this throughout your day and as often as you remember to do so.

Reinforce your actions by meditating, either a guided meditation specifically to enhance your psychic abilities or simply by your normal meditation. You absolutely must be open to receiving psychic messages and you must absolutely believe your intuition when you start hearing it.

So many people have what I refer to as "psychic dyslexia" or the feeling that they knew something was going to happen, but they didn't believe it so they were shocked when it did. I know, dyslexia is a reading impairment, but these people truly are impaired in their ability to read (and listen to) their psychic messages. Don't allow yourself to become one of these people.

If you are going to expend the effort of developing your psychic ability, please, put in the extra effort to allow yourself to actually listen and believe it.

Besides being psychic, many clients have asked me about how they can become mediums and talk to their deceased loved ones. Again, I do believe everyone has this ability, people either just cannot allow themselves to believe this is true or they are simply afraid of seeing ghosts so they don't allow themselves to see or hear what's already there.

For the most part, I have found that the deceased want to be able to communicate with us. They want us to know they're ok and that they're watching over us. They want us to know they still love us and they want us to be happy.

Sometimes there are earthbound spirits that are not happy and are not trying to reach a loved one, but these are not the ones I'm talking about here and that is a whole other story for a whole other book. Suffice it to say, if your grandmother loved roses and wore rose perfume and you occasionally get a very strong whiff of roses when there are no roses nearby...that is your grandmother saying hello and that she loves you.

I have a friend who lost her husband not too long after the birth of their son. Before he had died he liked to torment her with a particularly loud and annoying baby toy and one morning when she was having a very difficult time getting ready for work she heard this toy in the bathroom.

Knowing there was no one in the bathroom she was initially very frightened. Eventually she got up the nerve to go into the bathroom and see how this toy was making noise all by itself and upon entering the bathroom she noticed the toy on the counter by the sink and a distinct "kiss-print" on the mirror that wasn't there just a few minutes before.

Yes, the kiss print was just at the right height for her deceased husband to have put there. While she says she was still a little bit afraid, she also admitted it gave her a sense of comfort to feel like he was still watching out for her and their son.

You will find as you go further along your spiritual path that these messages seem to come along more frequently and you become aware that even when there's no one else around, you are still never really alone. I've known people who occasionally say "please leave me alone I need some privacy" out loud in their own homes, simply because they realize how very real this is.

Many of my clients are really interested in developing their ability to see auras, or the energy fields surrounding every living thing. I think the mistake most people make is that they are trying too hard.

This is one of those times when the harder you look the less you will see and I've found the best way to teach someone to see auras is really to close their eyes initially.

Usually, if you close your eyes and think of someone, really picture their face, think about what they're like and how you feel about them you will get at least an idea of a color. That color usually corresponds to the person's aura and will most likely be the predominant color.

Once you've tried this with your eyes closed and just visualizing the person, try it when they're right in front of you and you're actually looking at them. It works best in the beginning if they're standing or sitting in front of a blank wall, preferably a light colored one.

Look at the point between their eyes, or at the top of their head and let your focus soften so that you're not really seeing clearly. In your peripheral vision you should begin to see their aura. Do not try and look right at it because it will fade away.

You will find it takes a lot of practice to see auras, but once you do get the hang of it, you can see them everywhere. I can't tell you how many times I've had someone call to say they never realized their dog had an aura, but yes, every living thing does.

When you get really good at it, you will see the auras of complete strangers walking past you on the street. The world becomes a lot more colorful.

Astral projection or out of body experience is another thing people seem to really want to be able to do, and is also something I feel we're all born with. Really, I think the ability to meditate is the first step in learning astral projection and I really recommend you start there.

Get into as deep a meditation as you feel comfortable in and simply instruct yourself to have an out of body experience when you go to sleep that night. Like anything else this will take some practice, but if you tell yourself you will be safe and that nothing bad will happen to your body while you're out of it, you'll find you're able to have these experiences as often as you really want.

Fear is what stops most people from projecting out of their bodies and that is exactly what you should try to rid yourself of when you meditate for this purpose.

I have personally found astral projection to be immensely helpful when I'm trying to find a solution to a problem or need help working on a difficult project. Often your astral experiences will lead you right to whatever you are trying to find and you'll wake up with the solutions you've been looking for but were unable to find.

Usually, when I'm using astral projection for such a purpose I give myself instructions before I go to sleep that I want to go out and find whatever it is I'm looking for. If you are open to what you discover, you will realize that even though it probably isn't exactly what you were thinking, it is absolutely the correct answer to your problem.

Make sure you have cleared your mind of any negativity or apprehension related to the idea of astral projection before you attempt it. And make certain you give explicit instructions to yourself as to what you want to experience during your astral journey.

While it is very uncommon, it is not impossible that you could be lead into an entirely different adventure than the one you would prefer if your intentions are not clearly stated and positive. Most people do surround themselves with a bright white light of protection.

These are very brief overviews of psychic abilities and astral projection but if these subjects are of interest to you then you at least have a starting point for future discovery. And there are many other ways to use these abilities that those I've stated here.

We've all heard about those psychic mediums that assist various police agencies with missing person cases and murder cold cases and there's really no reason you couldn't develop your abilities to that extent and be one of those psychics yourself if you wanted to.

Two pebbles

Everyone has spirit guides, angels, familiars, elementals - whatever label you would like to attach to yours. They do not mind what we call them, and they don't even care if we acknowledge that they exist. These are beings made of pure love and light who exist solely to assist us. Learn to communicate with yours and you will be amazed at the difference it makes in your life.

I'm often asked how we go about communicating with these beings, and here is just one method I've taught others to do. You must always begin at the beginning, so instead of asking for complex answers to complex questions I teach people to ask simple "yes" or "no" questions at first.

The technique that I found to be the simplest for most people is to go outside and pick up the first two pebbles you are drawn to. The only criterion is that they fit well in your hand and they can fit into your pocket.

Of course, you could use crystals, sticks, or whatever else you choose. The point is to have two separate items, one of which will be your "yes" item and the other will be your "no." For this text, I will use the word "pebbles."

Start by closely examining your pebbles; notice how they are different or how they are similar. Feel the weight of each pebble in your hand; is it a smooth or rough pebble? Decide which of these will signify "yes" and which will be "no".

Hold your "yes" pebble and say the word "yes" to yourself, or out loud if you wish. Notice how the pebble feels as you say the word. Does it feel warm or cool? Does it seem to have a vibration to you? Whatever you feel is the right thing for you to be feeling, and it is ok if you feel nothing at all.

Now, do the same with your "no" pebble. Does it feel the same or different than the "yes" pebble? Many people have told me they feel a discernible difference in the energies between the two pebbles. If you do not, again, that is ok. Keep trying until you can tell the difference between the two pebbles without looking.

Once you've gone through this exercise choose a simple yes or no question to ask of your guides (or whatever you wish to call them). I usually advise people to choose an obvious question like "is the sky blue?" but any straightforward question that can be answered with yes or no will work.

Holding one pebble in each hand, close your eyes open your mind and ask your question. In my suggested question of "is the sky blue" you would feel drawn to the "yes" pebble. If I had asked "is my name Rufus Rastus?" I would feel drawn to the "no" pebble. As always, it is ok if you feel nothing the first few, or even several times.

Often it takes us a lot of practice to open our mind enough to actually feel the pebbles. However long it takes you is the right amount of time for you. Once you are able to feel the answers through your pebbles you are ready to move on to asking questions of your guides.

The first few times you try to communicate with your guides you may feel a little awkward and that is ok. With practice it will get easier and you will feel more comfortable.

First off, you will need a quiet place where you will not be disturbed. Many people prefer going outside, but you can just as easily be inside. Take several deep breaths and clear your thoughts. If you are familiar with meditating, this is what we're going for here.

Get comfortable, close your eyes and relax. Set a mental intention to communicate with your guides and formulate your yes or no question. With a pebble in each hand ask your question. You should feel drawn to one pebble or the other.

After a while, you will find you no longer need your pebbles in order to receive answers from your guides. Like any new skill, this takes a bit of practice. Eventually, you will become so proficient at seeking answers from your guides in time you will be able to simply ask a mental question and receive an answer.

Don't be frustrated if this takes a long time for you to do as there truly is no time-limit on learning to communicate with your guides. They will be there for you anyway.

Once you become adept at communicating with your guides you will come to realize that there are many different realms within our universe and that we are never truly alone.

While I know many people who find this idea frightening, really it should be comforting to know that there are loving beings that exist to help us along our way. I've been asked several times about spirits that don't really seem to have our best interest at heart, or about ghosts trying to possess someone and how do we tell the difference between these spirit beings and our angels, spirit guides etc.?

Basically, if you feel anything other than pure love and positive vibration coming from a spirit of any kind, immediately tell it to go away. Call in your guides if you need to, pray to whatever higher power you pray to or turn on lights and get a smudge stick if it comes to that. Do whatever you need to do to get rid of this negative entity.

As a rule of thumb I smudge my house with sage daily, this is not because I think I have any negative energy or negative spirits in my house it's simply to keep them from coming in. I work with a number of often troubled clients and through the years have found it much easier to prevent something negative from coming in than to get rid of something negative after it's already inside.

It should come as no surprise that you can also smudge yourself if you're feeling particularly negative. And I've recommended to various people that they should do this from time to time, if for no other reason than it makes them refocus on becoming positive and on getting rid of the negativity.

Afterward

By this point you should be well on your way to discovering your true spiritual path and to not only taking out your trash but filling that empty space with love and light. This book is intended to give you a base from which to grow and perhaps a direction in which to start your own journey. There is, of course, a whole lot more information that what is contained in these pages and I do hope you take the time to read more, learn more and discover more about yourself and this universe we are all a part of.

You may contact Kellie Fitzgerald or IbbiLane Press by visiting ibbilanepress.com.